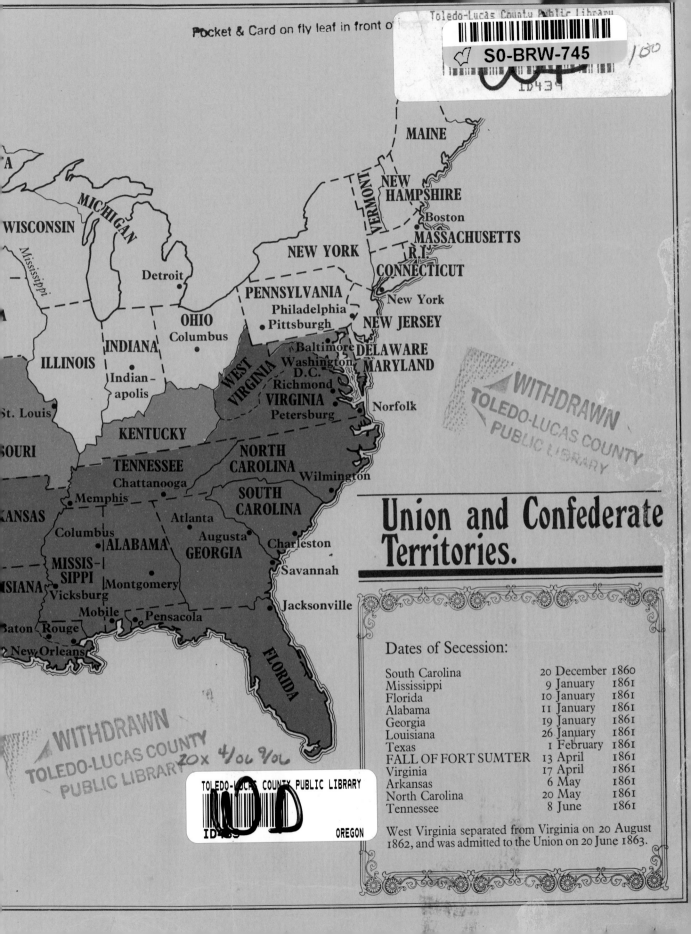

Union and Confederate Territories.

Dates of Secession:

South Carolina	20 December	1860
Mississippi	9 January	1861
Florida	10 January	1861
Alabama	11 January	1861
Georgia	19 January	1861
Louisiana	26 January	1861
Texas	1 February	1861
FALL OF FORT SUMTER	13 April	1861
Virginia	17 April	1861
Arkansas	6 May	1861
North Carolina	20 May	1861
Tennessee	8 June	1861

West Virginia separated from Virginia on 20 August 1862, and was admitted to the Union on 20 June 1863.

The American Civil War

G. Schomaekers

The American Civil War

Blandford Press Poole Dorset

Cover: The Battle of Gettysburg (July 1863). Detail from a painting by Paul Philippoteaux, Gettysburg National Military Park.

Frontispiece: General U. S. Grant at City Point (Virginia), the Potomac army's large supply depot during the siege of Petersburg.

This page: The gun turret of the *Monitor* after being bombarded by the Confederate *Virginia* during the first engagements between Ironclads in naval history, 9 March 1862.

ISBN 0 7137 0872 7

© 1976 Unieboek, Bussum, Holland
English translation by Anthony Kemp © 1977
Blandford Press, Link House, West Street, Poole,
Dorset BH15 1LL, England

Original title: Der amerikanische Bürgerkrieg
English edition first published 1977

Filmset in 'Monophoto' Times 10 on 12 pt. by
Richard Clay (The Chaucer Press), Ltd., Bungay,
Suffolk
and printed in Great Britain by
Fletcher & Son Ltd., Norwich

Contents

Introduction

The photograph on the preceding pages 6/7 demonstrates a typical aspect of the devastation incurred in the American Civil War. Here we see the ruins of Fort Sedgwick, Petersburg.

A mere 85 years after the Declaration of Independence by the United States of America, the young nation was convulsed by one of the greatest civil wars of modern times, but in spite of this the Union was preserved. The bitter struggle lasted four years, and is still clouded today by a certain aura of romance, although it cost the U.S.A. more casualties than both world wars.

For Americans the memory of this bitter war has still not paled, and hardly a week goes by without a new book on those eventful years being published. But apart from the events, we must consider the consequences. The Union was saved by President Lincoln and the armies of the North, but the problem of the Negroes in no small measure remains.

In 1861, the aim of the North was not to destroy the slave-based economy of the South, but to prevent the spread of it into the new territories and states. Two opposing camps, whose economies were based upon differing forms, and whose political views of the rights of individual states were irreconcilable, had 'confronted' each other for years. Following the election of Abraham Lincoln as the new President, it seemed that war was the only way out of a situation that no longer permitted of a negotiated compromise.

The population of the North did not go to war to free the slaves, but for the preservation of the Union. The former followed of its own accord after the advance of the Northern armies. As a result of their military occupation of the Southern rebel states, however, the Negro question came to a head. The slaves had left their masters and followed the Union armies who they regarded as their liberators.

President Lincoln had feared that Great Britain and France would intervene on behalf of the Confederacy, and because of this he issued the Declaration of Emancipation on 1 January 1863. Thus the intervention of the European powers was no longer morally feasible; the retention of slavery after all was an anachronism in the second half of the nineteenth century.

The assassination of President Lincoln on 14 April 1865 erased all hope of a favourable deal for the black population, who were now U.S. citizens. In fact, nobody really bothered about them, and matters were more or less allowed to slide.

The economy of the South, mainly based on the ownership of slaves, was destroyed as a result of the war, and a large proportion of the Negroes went North, where, however, they were barely tolerated especially by the White working class, being potentially substitute cheap labour. The mass of the Negroes though could neither read nor write, and thus could only perform the most menial and worst paid jobs.

In the South in the post-war years, the blacks were hated, as they were used by the Northern military governments as voters and to pack the legislative assemblies, where their voices dominated. The result was racial hatred, which had long-lasting results. In the States which had formed the Confederation from 1861 to 1865, you may still see the old Southern flag flying alongside the Stars and Stripes; a symbol of past glories as well as a token of continuing opposition to the rights of the Negroes.

The American Civil War was the first modern economic war. In Europe, however, no lessons were absorbed from this innovation or indeed from the conduct of military operations. The German General Staff, well known for its egocentricity, believed it unnecessary to learn from the war, and Field Marshal Helmut von Moltke was of the opinion that only 'armed mobs' had fought in America. Certainly, no soldiers fought on the American battlefields who had been trained by such brutal drill methods as the Prussian system. They were free men. Drill and unconditional obedience in those days were often confused by the European professional soldiers with strategy and tactics.

In many ways in method the American Civil War was a forerunner of the First World War. It demonstrated that on account of increased fire power, even large armies were no longer able to frontally assault strong and well-constructed enemy positions. Flank manoeuvre was possible, but the emphasis was developed on economic blockade and the strategy of attrition. The Southern states, economically the weaker side, were doomed to defeat as the Northern stranglehold became more powerful. For the first

8

The old flag of the Confederacy, which was introduced on 4 March 1861, consisted of a white horizontal band between two red ones. In the upper left hand corner was a circle of seven white stars on a blue field.

graphs that are valuable for the understanding of the war. The bulk of the pictures were taken by Union photographers; unfortunately little was taken by the South. Naturally the reader cannot expect action shots of the fighting, as this was technically impossible at the time. Posed pictures, taken after the battles, nevertheless often provide as deep an insight into events. This was also the first war to be photographed in any depth and the following pages provide a portentous record of the camera at war.

Guenter Schomaekers

time in modern history, it was an economic blockade rather than pure military strength – which as far as the North was concerned only became apparent towards the end – that led to total defeat of the South. Whichever side controlled the sea routes and could mobilize its industrial potential, even after early defeats, was destined to win.

The present work is not an attempt to provide a complete account of the war in all its military, political and economic aspects. This concept would have exceeded the scope of the book. It is more concerned with giving an overall unbiased view to the student of military history. The reader who wishes to study one or other of the campaigns in detail, or the political and social history, is referred to the bibliography. In view of the mass of literature concerning these war years, it has been impossible to quote everything, especially those works prior to 1900; but the most important works readily available in libraries have been listed.

The quantity of extant photographic material concerning the war is enormous. It has therefore been difficult to provide a representative selection. The author believes, however, that he has chosen photo-

Irreconcilable Opponents

Preceding pages. Another picture of static warfare. Union troops in the trenches at Petersburg.

The U.S.A. before the Civil War. The Industrial Revolution had started in the United States, as in the European Countries, before 1861. America was still a farming country however, but it was the last time in its history that agricultural products would exceed those of industry. Decisive for this situation was that in the U.S.A. prior to 1860, two social systems had developed – those of the North and of the South. Each tried to cope with the embryo industrialization in different ways, and even to further it. The resulting differences were heightened because of the slave economy of the South, so that it seemed impossible to reconcile the opposing views as to the future. A war-like settlement became increasingly imminent as the year 1861 approached.

Had it not been for the problem of slavery, it is probable that the Union would not have had to stand the strain of war. It was believed initially, that as had accrued in the North, slavery in the South would simply disappear of its own accord, as it was no longer a paying proposition. The discovery of the cotton gin machine, however, which made it possible to process the short cotton fibres, altered the situation completely. Cotton was in demand everywhere, and the Southern states could deliver enormous quantities, cheaply planted and harvested by slaves.

In 1860, the cotton exports of the U.S.A. had reached a value of 191 million dollars and represented 57 per cent. of the total exports of North America. Four million slaves ensured a healthy growth for the cotton kingdom of the South. Thus it seemed that slavery was essential for the economic existence of that part of the country, as well as for its political development.

The North was opposed to the institution of slavery, but had no concrete proposals as to how the system could be abolished without spelling financial ruin for the South. In this respect, one must bear in mind that the value of the slaves before 1861 was around two billion dollars. The reaction of the South to the abolition movement was to close ranks even more closely to defend the system.

The argument for and against slavery deepened the division between North and South. It became one of the main causes for the outbreak of the lengthy Civil War.

It was not only the argument about slavery that increasingly deepened the divisions between the two sections of the Union. Two social systems had developed, and each had differing ideas about the role of the State.

In the Northern harbours, hundreds of immigrants were arriving daily, the majority of whom moved off to the West where enormous areas of land could be obtained for cultivation. The newcomers founded industries and demanded protective customs tariffs against cheap imports from abroad – so that they could sell their manufactures at competitive prices internally. The communications networks enjoyed an enormous boom, and the ambitious society of the North demanded all sorts of help from the Federal government in Washington.

In the South, on the other hand, conditions were different. The society there was rigid and hardly altered. Immigration was minimal, as newcomers had only a slender chance to rise into the class of plantation owners. There were few towns and industrial growth remained modest.

While the North demanded tariff protection against cheap imports, the other part of the country wanted as many as possible. This opposing viewpoint also became with time insoluble. The South especially feared that with increasing Northern influence on the government in Washington, laws would be passed that would lead to their ruin. To protect themselves against this, the South developed the theory that each individual State had the right to declare any Federal law as unconstitutional, if it were believed to be detrimental to the interests of the State concerned. It should have been possible to settle such differences through a natural democratic development in the U.S.A., but this was hampered by the slavery question.

Various compromises were proposed before 1860 in an effort to find a peaceful solution to the problem. Both sides, however, were dissatisfied with such agreements. The situation became explosive on account of the Fugitive Slave Act of 18 November 1850. This was passed to oblige the South and provided for fugitive slaves to be returned to their owners. It caused great anger in the North, and resulted in a great gain of strength to the underground movement that assisted fleeing slaves to get into Canada. When in 1852, Harriett Beecher Stowe's *Uncle Tom's Cabin* was published – in the first year 300,000 copies were sold – tempers became increasingly heated in both parts of the country.

Kansas-Nebraska Act. Senator Stephen A. Douglas from Illinois, who was friendly towards the Southern viewpoint and not bothered by slavery, felt that a transcontinental railway should be built, running from Chicago to the West, thus crossing the North of the Union. To achieve this project, the land to the west of Iowa and Missouri had first to be surveyed and divided into new territories. As opposed to this, the South wanted the railway to be built from Texas through New Mexico to the Pacific. Senator Douglas thus needed the support of the Southern states to realize his plans. He therefore introduced in 1854, a bill to create the new territories of Kansas and Nebraska, whereby these States as soon as they were accepted into the Union, would decide for themselves whether slavery should be permitted or not. This meant that the Missouri Compromise of 1820 would no longer be valid, as this had laid down that to the north of latitude 36° 30′ (the southern border of Missouri), there would be no further slave states, with the exception of Missouri itself.

Because of this Act, public opinion in the North became even more entrenched in opposition to slavery. Both sides tried, especially in Kansas, to increase their influence even by using force. In the Senate, members insulted each other, and went as far as fighting with their walking sticks.

Abraham Lincoln. In this period of political upheaval, the two older American parties, the Whigs and the Democrats, went their own ways. As an offshoot of the developing Industrial Revolution in the North, the Republican party was founded. This attracted many previous supporters of the Whigs, as well as business men who demanded that industry be protected by Washington. More importantly, the lower classes supported the Republicans, from whom they expected a homestead law to provide them with free land in the West.

Various Republican candidates, among them Abraham Lincoln, hoped to become President at the next election. He came from a poor family, and was born on 12 February 1802 in a log cabin in Hodgeville, Kentucky, where he lived for seven years 13

Abraham Lincoln (1809–65), 16th President of the United States. Photographed in the White House with his son Thomas (Ted) while reading the Bible.

Lincoln lost the election, he was by then well known and could aspire to the Presidency.

In the summer of 1857, the U.S.A. suffered another deep economic crisis, so that in the North the demands for higher tariffs and a homestead law became louder. The South, however, was hardly affected by the crisis, which served to strengthen their view that as cotton was still in demand, their system was more stable than that of the North. The government in Washington almost came to a standstill on account of the deepening division between the two parties, especially as the President, James Buchanan (1857–61), showed great sympathy for the South.

On 16 October 1859, the ardent abolitionist John Brown, with a few followers attacked the Federal arsenal at Harpers Ferry, in order to start a slave insurrection in the South with the weapons that they had captured. He was arrested, however, and executed the following December, but his action made a great impression in both parts of the country – although John Brown was more a small-time guerrilla than a military hero. The South believed, though, that the northern Yankees planned an uprising, while in the North, Brown's posthumous fame at least was immortalized in the folk song on the lips of Northern troops.

Thus the political situation in the Union by 1860 was strained to breaking point. In addition, it was an election year, and Lincoln was nominated as the candidate of the Republican party. He had been selected because he was not an extremist, took a mild view of the slavery question, and most importantly, was of the opinion that the Federal government did not have the power to interfere in individual States. For the South, however, the election of a Republican was a threat, in that the party favoured an increase in the tariffs, free farms in the West and the building of the railway in the North.

Lincoln won the election by a slender majority, although he had not involved himself personally in the campaign. The Republicans received 1,866,452 votes, the Democrats (Southern Democrats) 847,953 votes, and finally the Constitutional Union party 590,631 votes. The Southern states feared the worst, although there were no particular grounds for this. Abraham Lincoln, the new President, had not the slightest intention of abolishing slavery by force.

until the family moved to Indiana. He had no formal schooling, as life on the frontiers was far too hard to bother with such things. Thus he educated himself while following a variety of occupations – waggon driver, sailor, shopkeeper, etc. In 1830 the family moved to Illinois, where they lived in New Salem.

He took part in frontier wars against the Indians, became Postmaster, and in 1837 was finally admitted as a lawyer. From 1847–8 he was a member of the House of Representatives, and enjoyed a good reputation as a lawyer. In 1854, he again became involved in political life, and opposed the extension of slavery, although not the institution itself. In 1856 he joined the Republicans, and two years later he tried for the Senatorship of Illinois against the famous Stephen A. Douglas. Both argued about the Kansas-Nebraska Act and the question of slavery, in speeches that have since become famous. Although

The secession of the South. It was South Carolina that was the first State to leave the Union, this far-reaching step being prepared by the Legislative Assembly, and on 20 December 1860, they declared that the Union was thus dissolved. One State alone could not have maintained itself, but the other Cotton states soon followed – 9.1.61 Mississippi, 10.1.61 Florida, 11.1.61 Alabama, 19.1.61 Georgia, 26.1.61 Louisiana, 1.2.61 Texas, 17.4.61 Virginia, 6.5.61 Arkansas, 20.5.61 North Carolina and 8.6.61 Tennessee.

Had the others not followed the example of South Carolina, Washington could have used force to coax her back into the fold, and in the South there would have been no more talk of secession.

Opposed to the eleven States who had left the Union were – Maine, Vermont, New Hampshire, Massachusetts, Rhode Island, Connecticut, New York, New Jersey, Pennsylvania, Ohio, Indiana, Illinois, Iowa, Michigan, Wisconsin, Minnesota, California, Oregon, Missouri, Kentucky, Maryland, Delaware. The last four States had a slave economy, but

remained in the Union or were kept by force from seceding.

The Southern states met together on 4 February 1861 in Montgomery, to form a provisional government. Four days later the constitution of the provisional government of the Confederate States of America was adopted, and on 9 February, the assembly elected Jefferson Davis as their new President.

Jefferson Davis was born in Kentucky in 1808, into a family of small farmers. He studied at the West Point Military Academy from where he passed out in 1828. After serving in minor army posts in Wisconsin and Illinois, he resigned from the service to live in retirement as a slave owner and planter in Missouri. During this period of his life, Jefferson Davis occupied himself with political ideas and theory. In 1845 he became a senator, after which he served in the war against Mexico. From 1853 to 1857, Davis was War Minister under President Franklin Pierce, and was regarded as one of the most capable incumbents of that office. Later, he

THE MAIN CAMPAIGN AREAS OF THE CIVIL WAR.

15

again became a senator, and in his speeches defended the right of individual States to leave the Union at any time. At the beginning of the secession he had hoped to become the commander of the Southern army, as he regarded himself as an efficient and capable general.

There was still concern that the approaching conflict should be settled peacefully. Especially Senator John T. Wittenden from Kentucky tried to reach an agreement on the basis of the Missouri Compromise, but Lincoln refused this as it would have perpetuated slavery as an institution. Thus the last chance to avoid a civil war passed. From then on it was only a question of who would open fire first.

Jefferson Davis (1808–89), President of the Confederacy. Davis was not really equal to his task. He was no great personality and did not possess sufficient skill to lead the Southern states through such difficult times. He was unable to settle the differences within the Confederacy about the army and the mobilization of reserves, and thus could not prevent the final Union conquest.

The first shots are fired – Fort Sumter. Previously there had been only political differences of opinion between South and North, and neither side really believed that the other, in order to realize their ideas and philosophy, would resort to force. Each thought that the other was only bluffing. Nobody took Abraham Lincoln seriously when in his inauguration speech he said that he would secure, occupy and defend all Federal property in the South. In his speech, Lincoln specifically referred to Fort Sumter, which was situated on an island in the entrance to Charleston Harbor (South Carolina).

Major Robert Anderson commanded the Union forces in Charleston, and on account of the tense situation, he withdrew from Fort Moultrie to Fort Sumter during the night of 26 February 1861. He had under his command more than seventy-six officers and men, plus forty-three civilian workmen, and had enough supplies to hold out for several weeks before being relieved.

The Stars and Stripes flying from Moultrie was an insult to the Confederation, which urged Washington to evacuate the place. On 5 January, the steamer *Star of the West* had left New York with soldiers on board to reinforce the Sumter garrison. In the meanwhile, the Confederates had erected batteries around the fort, and on 9 January, they opened fire on the *Star of the West*, forcing it to turn back. Brigadier-General P. G. T. Beauregard commanded the Southern forces in Charleston, and he demanded the evacuation of the fort on 10 April, which Anderson refused on the following day.

At about 04.30 hours on the morning of 12 April, the Confederate batteries opened fire, but some three hours elapsed before the fort replied. Subsequently it became apparent that the fort was insufficiently equipped for serious defence, and as the ammunition stocks were low, only a few guns answered. On the same day, the U.S. warship *Pawnee* and cutter *Harriet Lane* appeared off Charleston, accompanied by the steamer *Baltic*, but there was no longer anything that they could do. The fort was on fire, so that the garrison could no longer defend it. Anderson surrendered the following day, and with his troops was evacuated by the U.S. Navy on 14 April. As a result of the bombardment, two soldiers were killed and one was wounded. The first Union casualties of the Civil War had been incurred. While in the Confederate states there was immediate joy at the

When, following the election of Lincoln as President, the Southern states were considering leaving the Union, the loyal Major Robert Anderson made himself master of Fort Sumter which controlled the entrance to Charleston Harbor.

Major Robert Anderson, who was regarded in the North as a hero. On 13 April 1861, Anderson had to surrender the burning Fort Sumter, which he had defended for 34 hours against greatly superior Confederate numbers.

victory, in the North it was realized that the years of tension and indecision were over. The population of both sides now welcomed the conflict. Nobody realized that it would be fought until the South was completely exhausted; nowadays the enormity of this internecine war may be assessed by the knowledge that the combined casualties exceeded those for the U.S.A. in both world wars.

When he heard the news of the evacuation of Fort Sumter, President Lincoln declared that the powerful combination that had seized control in certain States in the South could not be defeated by the normal machinery of government. To restore order and dissolve the dangerous conspiracy, Lincoln proclaimed a State of Insurrection, and on 11 April called for 75,000 men to serve for three months to defeat the rebellion. The North rushed to the

colours, but with the result that Virginia, Tennessee and Arkansas left the Union – all States that up until then had hoped for a peaceful solution.

On 6 March, President Jefferson Davis had already made an appeal for 100,000 volunteers to serve for one year. By the middle of April 1861, 35,000 men were under arms, a force that was twice as large as the active U.S. Army.

Neither side had made military preparations for the conflict. Neither was there any idea of just what demands would be made by the war.

Preliminary Strategy

The armies of the North and the South. At the beginning of 1861, the U.S. Army totalled 16,367 officers and men. These, however, were so spread out all over the country that a mobilization of this small and unimportant force was pointless. It was the same with the Navy, and only a few ships were ready for sea.

Even if it had been possible to concentrate the Union army and to send it to war as a body, it would hardly have been able to force a decision. It was clear that the burden of the coming struggle would have to be borne by volunteers, initially the militia. There were, however, not enough weapons and uniforms to equip the new army, or sufficient skilled personnel to act as officers. The actual militia had little military value, and its training was regarded as being of a low standard – once a year there was a muster, more of a parade than a military manoeuvre. On top of this, the militia was unable to execute any battle evolutions, for example, changing from column of march into line, especially in regimental formations.

Each company wore the uniform that it preferred and the officers were elected by the men. Many of them owed their position either to political influence or to the fact that they were prominent citizens. Few of them had the basic qualities of leadership, and only in battle was it found out who was suitable. One could say for the North, as well as for the South, that initially amateurs were led by amateurs. The experiences of the first months of the war were studied only hesitantly, especially in the North, and it was only with the end of the struggle that the Union crushed the Confederacy with its enormous superiority in manpower and materials.

For the first time, the enormous and inexhaustible economic potential of the United States was demonstrated. It needed much more time, however, to establish the economy on a war footing, but once mobilized, the enemy was simply overpowered by superior force.

The Army and Navy of the Union, like the country as a whole, were affected by the secession. Regular soldiers, who served for a certain period, either remained in the army or deserted. Less than fifty soldiers and sailors, however, chose the latter course. For officers it was different. They could simply resign their commissions, and many took the opportunity to do so.

Of the 1,036 officers, 286 resigned to serve in the Southern armies, while from the 1,300 naval officers, some 200 joined the Confederate forces. Those who decided to leave the Regular army remained in their positions to the last, in order to formally hand over their commands.

The Commander-in-Chief of the Union Army was Winfield Scott, who was already 75 years old, and proved to be no longer capable of exercising the responsibility. He had served with distinction in earlier campaigns; especially in the war with Mexico. He had been Commander-in-Chief since 1841, and in 1855, as the second American officer (besides George Washington), had been promoted to Lieutenant-General. Scott realized right at the beginning of the war just what efforts were required to defeat the South. He immediately suggested a blockade of the Confederacy and supported the raising of an army of 300,000 men. As soon as these could be equipped and trained, he planned to march down the Mississippi to the Gulf of Mexico. In this operation, the Army in the west and the Navy in the east would isolate the Southern states from the outside world.

The thought of a long and bloody war was regarded as heresy in Washington. The politicians demanded a cheap and speedy victory, without considering how it could be achieved without the necessary means being available. General Scott's plan, known as the Anaconda Plan on account of its similarity to a snake choking its victim, was not approved. In spite of this, the plan was later carried out by the Union, although not quite as originally conceived. The South, however, did eventually capitulate to the stranglehold of the Northern snake.

At first, the Union had no really clear idea as to how to employ their officers in the best way. In the South, on the other hand, they were more astute. President Jefferson Davis may have regarded himself as more of an expert in the art of war than he actually was, but he gave commands as far as possible to efficient and experienced officers.

Right from the outset, the South had available a number of gifted generals, such as Robert E. Lee, Pierre Gustave Toutant Beauregard, Albert Sidney Johnston and Joseph (Joe) Eggleston Johnston. All the generals on both sides knew each other from the days before 1861, as the Army had been so small. Their tactical and strategic decisions, therefore, were to a certain extent influenced by their knowledge of their opponents.

The war aims of both the North and the South were simple and straightforward. The North was fighting for the preservation of the Union, while the South was demanding its independence. The Confederacy, therefore, went on to the defensive and did not attack the Union; the North in the role of the aggressor kept up the offensive in order to achieve its aims and win the war. It had to mobilize all the advantages that it possessed in the way of manpower and economic wealth to be able to mount such an offensive over a period of time.

Requirements for a Northern victory. Taking the figures of the 1860 census, there lived in the North 18,936,579 Whites, while in the States that had left the Union, there were only 5,449,467. To these could be added the 2,589,533 Whites in the slave states of Delaware, Kentucky, Maryland and Missouri which had remained in the Union but sympathized with the South. If one subtracted the population of Virginia and Tennessee which had remained loyal, then there were some five million Whites in the Confederacy plus 3,521,111 Negro slaves. The latter belonged to 384,000 Whites, only 1,800 of whom owned more than 100 Negroes. In the above mentioned four Northern Slave states, there were 429,401 Negroes. These so-called Frontier states provided the Union with 100,000 soldiers during the war.

90 per cent. of the economy of the United States was concentrated in the North, which also had the use of two-thirds of the railway network including all the factories and workshops for building and repairing locomotives, rolling stock and permanent way equipment.

In contrast to the South, the North was rich in minerals, including iron, coal, copper etc. It produced enormous quantities of foodstuffs, especially corn, that was exported to Europe, and the income from this was used to procure munitions.

Just how much of a disadvantage was suffered by the South, is demonstrated by a comparison with the State of New York, which produced goods four times as high in value as the whole of the manufactures of the South.

The foregoing did not necessarily mean that victory would automatically be gained by the Union. It first had to invade the South, and as in all wars, the attacker had to have superiority in manpower and material. The Confederation only needed to remain on the defensive until the North became weary of the struggle. To win the war, the Union had to conquer an area that was as large as Western Europe. The South was defending its own territory, with the geography of which it was well acquainted, while the Northern troops were fighting for an abstract ideal that could easily become faded as soon as war-weariness set in.

Kentucky, Maryland and Missouri. Right from the outset, Abraham Lincoln was faced with the difficult problem of keeping the frontier states within the Union, a requirement for a final Union victory. Kentucky was ruled by a secessionist Governor, while the Legislative Assembly favoured the North. Thus the position was stalemate, but though Kentucky officially decided on neutrality, this did not prevent the State from becoming a battleground, and troops were illegally recruited by both sides there.

In Maryland there was much sympathy for the Confederation, but after a regiment that was marching through Baltimore on 19 April 1861 had been fired on, Washington resorted to force. The members of the Legislative Assembly who favoured the South were arrested and imprisoned.

Missouri was also held in the Union by military force, although the Confederates were able to establish themselves in the south-western part of the territory.

The western part of Virginia remained loyal to the North, left the Confederation, and as West Virginia, joined the Union as a new State on 30 June 1863. These successes did not benefit the Union all that much at the time, and the Confederacy continued with its plans to resist invasion. Since 20 July 1861, the Congress of the Southern states had been meeting at Richmond, Virginia, and troops were assembled to defend the city.

Early Union Defeats

Preceding pages. On 14 February 1862, four Ironclads and two gun-boats, commanded by Andrew H. Foote, attacked Fort Donelson on the Cumberland River, but were unable to silence it. The ships were forced to withdraw heavily damaged.

The first Battle of Bull Run. If Lieutenant-General Scott had had his way, the first year of the war would have been spent in training and equipping the army. He regarded it as irresponsible to start the offensive with insufficiently trained volunteer troops. From a military point of view, he was right, but in the American Civil War, political motives often influenced events to a greater extent than was required by logic.

The Confederacy behaved more prudently, but militarily found themselves in a hopeless state. Thousands of soldiers volunteered, most of whom had previous experience with handling weapons, but which the Army could not supply them with in sufficient quantities.

At the beginning of hostilities, the U.S. arsenals were stocked with 560,000 smooth-bore muskets and 49,000 breech-loading rifles, and of these, respectively 260,000 and 22,000 fell into the hands of the Confederacy. These quantities were insufficient for equipping the armies of the Southern states especially as many of the weapons dated from the time of the War of Independence – 110,000 fully obsolete models.

The Confederacy could easily have coped with the shortage of weapons if they had exported cotton in large quantities to Europe. The U.S. Navy blockade was not as efficient as it would later become, and the proceeds could have been used for the purchase of all types of weapons. The South believed, however, in the slogan of 'King Cotton', and imagined that if they withheld supplies from England and France, those countries would intervene on their behalf and finally recognize the independence of the Confederacy. They therefore committed the fatal mistake of keeping back their cotton in the early decisive months of the war, so that England and France would be hit by the shortage (80 per cent. of their imports came from the U.S.A.). Neither power reacted as expected, however, and on 13 April 1861 England declared her neutrality, followed by France on 10 June and Spain on 17 June.

The Southern states had overlooked the fact that as a result of recent good harvests, there was an excess of cotton, and that especially England had enough in stock for quite some time – more than 50 per cent. of her normal requirements. It was also forgotten that she could import cotton from Egypt and India, as well as the Union itself! In the years 1860–65, the latter sent five million bales to England, and both England and France took the opportunity of processing their excess quantities to make themselves independent of North America. At the same time, the Confederacy was firmly of the opinion that the English workers, who were the hardest hit by these measures, would exert pressure in favour of the South on their government. Although in the winter of 1861 some 330,000 cotton operatives were out of work, those from Manchester assured President Lincoln that the interests of the Union were the same as theirs. Throughout Europe, the working classes supported the Union, as a victory for the latter would be a victory for democracy.

Thus in 1861, the armaments situation of the Southern armies was not particularly favourable, but with time this could be made good to a certain extent by their own production. Also, in spite of the blockade, a certain number of weapons were brought in from overseas.

A view of Harpers Ferry on the Potomac which occupied a key position in West Virginia. This was the main Union arsenal, and when it was evacuated on 18 April 1861, the machinery was only partly destroyed, so that much of it was carried off by the Confederates.

In the majority of the battles of the Civil War, the Union was on the losing side, and thus the Confederacy, especially in 1862, was able to capture enormous quantities of armaments – in that year some 100,000 rifles and the same number in 1863. After then, however, the armaments situation became critical and a shortage of all types of weapons made itself felt.

Initially, the Union troops were poorly organized and trained, but were far better equipped with weapons. Up until the middle of 1862, the North spent ten million dollars on rifles, carbines etc. These included 116,750 Enfield rifles, 48,108 from France, 170,255 from Austria, 111,549 from Prussia, 57,194 from Belgium and a further 203,831 from other countries.

The standard equipment of a Union soldier mostly included the Enfield rifle, of which some 250,000 were purchased in Britain before their own production could supply their needs. There was also the famous Springfield rifle, manufactured at the Springfield arsenal in Massachusetts. In 1864, the Union produced almost 300,000 rifles, part of a grand total of 793,434 between January 1861 and the end of 1865.

The first major encounters of the Civil War resulted from the engagements fought by Major-General George Brinton McClellan, who advanced eastwards from West Virginia with 20,000 men. On 3 June

The small river Bull Run, scene of the first battle of the Civil War on 21 July 1861. The Union troops were defeated, but their opponents were unable to exploit the victory.

1861, 1,500 Confederates were put to flight, and on 11 July, 553 officers and men surrendered at Rich Mountain. McClellan reported that he had destroyed two armies, as a result of which the Union command thought that the troops camped around Washington under Brigadier-General Irwin, in spite of their poor training, should be able to defeat the Confederates between Washington and Richmond.

On 1 June Major-General McDowell was ordered to advance against and destroy the Confederate army

Pierre Gustave Toutant de Beauregard (1818–93), the Confederate general who played a part in most of the important events of the Civil War. He commanded the forces which bombarded Fort Sumter; took part at Bull Run; had the tactical command at Shiloh; led the defence of Charleston and at the end of the war achieved the southerly withdrawal from Richmond. Later, he made a small fortune as a railway director and as manager of the Louisiana lottery.

25

under Brigadier-General P. G. T. Beauregard, which had massed around Manassas Junction, an important railway centre. Manassas is some 27 miles from Washington and lies behind the Bull Run stream. In spite of protests that the Army was not yet ready for an offensive, the order was confirmed, as the reason for the decision to attack was based on the fact that after three months the militia would have returned to their homes. It had been agreed, therefore, to quickly use the available time for a blow at the Confederacy.

Lieutenant-General Thomas Jonathan Jackson (1824–63), nick-named 'Stonewall' Jackson, was one of the most important and most capable Confederate generals. On account of his unusual energy (which he failed to demonstrate during the Seven Day Battle at Richmond), his daring tactical manoeuvres and the efforts that he demanded from his men, he continually managed to defeat his Union opponents. This almost Prussian general from the Southern States was shot in the arm through a mistake by his own troops at the Battle of Chancellorsville on 2 May 1862. As the result of the consequent amputation and pneumonia, Jackson died on 10 May.

Near Harpers Ferry on the Potomac were positioned 16,000 Union troops commanded by Major-General Robert Patterson, and opposite him were some 12,000 Confederates under Major-General Joseph E. Johnston. Patterson's orders were to put pressure on the Confederates to prevent them from sending reinforcements to Beauregard or from uniting with him. The latter had more than 20,000 men behind the Bull Run, and McDowell was to attack Beauregard because his army blocked the advance of the Union troops in the direction of Richmond. If Patterson managed to destroy Johnston's position, it was thought that the superior numbers of the Union Army (30,600 men) stood a good overall chance of winning a decisive victory.

On 16 June, McDowell started his march and reached Centreville two days later. He should have immediately attacked on the following day when he would still have had a chance of winning, but his lines of communication were so bad that he dare not risk anything. His officers were too inexperienced to judge the situation, and in addition, the discipline of the militia troops was appalling.

McDowell's army left Washington as a colourful parade, each regiment sporting its own uniform. The baggage train was vast, and the soldiers left their columns to drink from streams and springs. They picked berries and sheltered from the searing heat under trees.

Brigadier-General Beauregard was well informed about the enemy advance, not only through excellent espionage, but on account of the fact that the Northern newspapers studiously reported the Union plans.

Beauregard wanted to push his right wing over the Bull Run to attack the left flank of McDowell before the latter had formed his order of battle. For his part, McDowell proposed to cross the stream and force back the left flank of the Confederates.

On 18 June, a division of the Union army that attempted a demonstration on the Potomac was driven off with light casualties, which greatly raised Confederate morale. Joe Johnston was encouraged accordingly to transport 9,500 men by railway to Manassas, where they arrived on 20 June.

The actual battle began the following day. McDowell succeeded in crossing the Bull Run to attack

Major-General George Brinton McClellan (1826–85) commanded the Potomac Army from 20 August 1861 to 5 October 1862. Although this army was always stronger than Robert E. Lee's Army of North Virginia, McClellan failed to produce a victory with the well equipped Union force. He was a good organizer and popular with his men, but always hesitant. He continually complained that Washington did not back him up sufficiently.

the Confederate left flank which he intended to throw back. His opponents, however, fought steadily until Johnston and Beauregard on the right arrived with reinforcements. Two well-trained Union batteries opened fire and the infantry advanced towards the wooded Henry House Hill, with the result that the Confederates began to weaken. A Virginian brigade under Brigadier-General Thomas Jonathan Jackson stood firm, however, and Brigadier-General Barnard Bee, who had collected some of the shattered Confederate regiments, cried out at that moment: 'there stands Jackson like a stone wall'. From that time onwards, he was known only as Stonewall Jackson, and proved to be one of the most capable Confederate commanders.

Jackson, born in Clarksburg, Virginia, passed out from West Point in 1846, and proved his capabilities in the Mexican war. In 1851, however, he resigned from the Army and lectured at the Virginia Military Institute. At the beginning of the Civil War he was promoted to Brigadier-General and sent to Harpers Ferry.

In the meanwhile, the Confederates had stabilized their front and were receiving regular reinforcements from Johnston, whose troops were thrown straight into the battle as they arrived from their trains. Both Union batteries were captured, as their crews thought that those attacking them belonged to their own side. This was because the Confederates were wearing blue uniforms, which later became the Northern colour, while the South wore grey.

At around 4 o'clock in the afternoon, the Union troops at first withdrew in an orderly fashion, but when they got back over the Bull Run, their retreat turned into a rout. This was partly caused by the battle spectators from Washington, and partly through the inexperience of the troops who did not understand how to withdraw and form into column. The visitors from Washington who wanted to witness the expected victory and who had organized picnics, rapidly fled from the field when they saw the retreating soldiers. At that moment a Confederate shell exploded on a bridge which resulted in a terrible panic. Soldiers and civilians tried to struggle across or force a way through on either side, and the situation became even worse when the shout went up that the Confederate cavalry was coming. The Yankees threw away their weapons – all wanted to be the first to reach the Potomac. By evening, McDowell's army no longer existed.

The Southerners were in no condition to organize a pursuit, as they were just as exhausted as the Northern troops, added to which their officers did not have enough experience to exploit the triumph. There was general satisfaction that a victory had been gained as well as a large quantity of booty.

The losses on the Union side were around 418 killed, while the Confederates suffered 387 dead. The figures seemed extraordinarily high for that time, although later both sides had to get used to much higher numbers.

Disillusionment came quickly. There was no more romantic talk. The militia had had its day and its value was non-existent. From then on both sides realized that they had to prepare for a long war.

In the South, there was temporary euphoria on account of the victory – a victory that was in fact of no account. From then on the Yankees were regarded by the Rebs as poor fighters and soldiers, and a final Confederate victory was confidently expected, all of which proved to be a dangerous underestimation on their part.

Before the next campaign could be initiated, however, the Union was acutely conscious that they had to establish a battle-worthy army, and bring organization, discipline and training up to the highest standard.

The beginning of the real war. As a result of the lost Battle of Bull Run, President Lincoln appointed Major-General George Brinton McClellan to command the Potomac army. McClellan, who was born at Philadelphia in 1826, had been the second-best cadet of the class of 1846 at West Point. He took part in the Mexican war and went to the Crimea as an observer. In 1857 he left the army and became chief engineer and vice-president of the Illinois Central Railway, and later president of the Ohio and Mississippi Railroad. When the war broke out, he assumed command of the Department of Ohio, and on 11 July, won the unimportant victory already described over the Confederates at Rich Mountain in West Virginia. He understood, nevertheless, how to exploit this action for the purposes of self propaganda.

The Union believed that in McClellan they had found the right man to defeat the South. He proved to be a brilliant organizer and trainer of soldiers, besides which he had some capabilities as a strategist. His failing was that he constantly tended to overestimate the strength of his opponents, so that he never dared the ultimate stroke. He was vain, convinced of his own capabilities and believed himself to be a Napoleon. His soldiers, however, loved him and would literally go through fire for him. Such popularity was achieved by no other Union general during the Civil War, not even by Grant, who was regarded as impersonal.

After Bull Run, both sides paused for breath. The Confederates were of the opinion that the Union would take the next step, although in fact, they were hardly capable of immediate combat.

In the meanwhile, the Southern states fortified their positions around Manassas, and General Joe Johnston erected dummy batteries to deter the Northern troops from attacking. The Confederates also fortified the southern bank of the Potomac, so that in the summer and autumn of 1861, they had almost isolated Washington from this waterway. Stonewall Jackson was stationed with a division of infantry in the Shenandoah Valley.

During this time the North was reorganizing its forces. The militia was abolished, and its members who were only obliged to serve for three months, were sent home. McClellan was planning a national army, to be made up of volunteer regiments which would serve for three years, combined with the small regular force. Although these would be Federal troops, the governors of the individual states exerted great influence on the formation of these regiments. Washington ordered the governor con-

cerned to set up a certain number of units, whereby he was responsible for the recruiting. Over and above this, the governor could exert political influence in that he had the right to nominate the officers. The system was cumbersome, but it functioned reasonably satisfactorily in 1861.

Throughout the North military camps were springing up, full of men exercising and drilling. Parades were held and McClellan inspected the newly raised regiments. The army gradually began to assume form, and in Washington the government began to breathe more easily.

The over cautious McClellan did not think in terms of a swift resumption of the campaign in Virginia: he wanted everything to be ready first; and anyway, he was of the opinion that the Confederates outnum-

Lieutenant-General Winfield Scott (1786–1866) since 1841 had been Commander-in-Chief of the U.S. Army. The 75-year-old general was forced to retire on account of his age. The illustration shows his last meeting with the cabinet.

bered his troops. In this supposition he was supported by the famous detective, Allan Pinkerton, who was in charge of the secret service. The latter's intelligence during the course of the Civil War was mostly false, and he always overestimated the Confederate numbers.

Meanwhile, the Union undertook a reconnaissance over the Potomac on 21 October. Several regiments crossed the river, but were ambushed at Ball's Bluff, a small wooded hill, and scattered. The Confederates took 714 prisoners, while 48 were killed and 158 wounded. In turn, the Rebs only lost 33 dead.

Militarily, the raid was unimportant, but it served as an excuse to do nothing further as far as the Union was concerned, until they felt themselves to be strong enough to attack.

General Winfield Scott was too old to continue to command the army, and he finally yielded to pressure to retire. On 1 November, McClellan was appointed as his successor, whereby as Commander-in-Chief he retained his command over the Potomac army.

The war in the West. After the first battles, in summer 1861 there was no further fighting of a serious

Ulysses Simpson Grant (1822–85) and George Gordon Meade (1815–72), respectively Commander-in-Chief of the U.S. Army and Commander of the Potomac army. They worked well together to lead the Union to the final victory.

nature in that year in Virginia. During this time, however, decisive events were happening in the West of the U.S.A., and there, the Union secured a number of advantages that were to prove important for the onward course of the war.

At Cairo, Illinois, where the Ohio flows into the Mississippi, Union troops were ready to advance south, either along the giant river, or following the lesser streams of the Cumberland and the Tennessee. Major-General John Charles Frémont commanded the newly created Western Department, but could not master the situation. Therefore he was relieved of his command by President Lincoln on 2 November, on the grounds of incompetence and disobedience. In spite of his previous lack of success, Frémont had initiated two things that were to be important for the future. He started to build gunboats, and appointed Brigadier-General Ulysses Simpson Grant to command the troops in Cairo.

Grant came from Ohio where he was born on 27 April 1822 in Point Pleasant. He commenced his military career on 30 May 1839 when he entered the famous military academy at West Point. At the beginning of the Civil War, nobody would have thought that Grant, together with Lee from the Confederacy, would achieve such fame. When Grant left West Point in 1843 he had himself achieved nothing whereby he could be remembered, although in the Mexican war he demonstrated great bravery. After the war he served on the West Coast, but during that time, without his family, he neglected his duties and began to drink. Because of this weakness he left the army in 1854 – to avoid being courtmartialled. Between then and the outbreak of the Civil War he had tried his hand at several professions without success, but when President Lincoln called for volunteers in 1861, U. S. Grant reported for duty. At first he was employed as Colonel of the 21st Illinois Regiment, but in August 1861 he assumed command in Cairo as Brigadier-General. The commander of the Confederate forces in West Tennessee was Major-General Leonidas Polk.

Polk (born in 1806 at Raleigh in North Carolina) had passed out of West Point in 1827, but left the army six months later to study theology. He became a bishop in Louisiana, but joined the Confederate Army on 25 June 1861 in the rank of major-general. Polk realized that the Union would occupy 'neutral' Kentucky, and therefore on 4 November occupied

Columbus and fortified the heights above the Mississippi. Thereupon Grant, supported by gunboats, captured Paducah, at the junction of the Tennessee and the Ohio rivers. Thus it was that Kentucky became a theatre of war. President Jefferson Davis had appointed Major-General Albert Sidney Johnston, a talented officer, as commander of the Department of the West – to which belonged Tennessee, West Mississippi (east of the river), Missouri, Arkansas and the Indian territories to the west.

Although Johnston had only 45,000 men at his disposal – as opposed to 65,000 Union troops – he concentrated 20,000 men around Columbus and fortified the bank of the river to keep it under his control. The rest of his troops, some 25,000 men, were camped in or around Bowling Green. Important for the defence of the South were the Cumberland and the Tennessee, which formed a gateway leading to the states of Tennessee, Alabama and Mississippi. As the Confederates had occupied Columbus, the Union would have to advance along the two former rivers.

To deny the use of this route to the Union forces, the Confederates had built Fort Henry on the Tennessee and Fort Donelson on the Cumberland.

Brigadier-General Grant and Andrew H. Foote, commander of the Mississippi flotilla, had realized right from the beginning that they could use the large western rivers as operational lines, whereby the Army and Navy would have to co-operate closely.

At the beginning of 1862, Grant was ordered to advance on Fort Henry and capture it, using 15,000 men and the new Ironclads (armoured river gunboats). The fort was nothing more than a field work, situated near the bank of the Tennessee, which was defended by one hundred men and seventeen guns, under the command of Brigadier-General Lloyd Tilghman.

On 6 February 1862, the gun-boats were deployed in front of Fort Henry, which was partly under floodwater, and after a short bombardment Tilghman surrendered. Grant's troops, who had been held up by the bad weather, no longer needed to take part in the action.

Grant then immediately marched east to Fort Donelson, and only a week after the loss of Fort Henry, the attack started. Johnston had decided, as

a result of the surrender of Fort Henry, to withdraw the Kentucky army to the south, but to cover this movement he wanted to hold Fort Donelson at all costs. He therefore sent more than 15,000 men there to reinforce the garrison.

On 14 February, Foote's gun-boats opened the bombardment, but were driven off, while on land, the struggle lasted three days before the Confederates surrendered to Grant on 16 February. For the first time, Grant was noted for his severe terms, the spirit of which was to be adopted by the Union as their main war strategy – 'no conditions other than immediate and unconditional surrender can be accepted'.

Grant's victory had wide ranging results. The Confederates had to evacuate the areas of Kentucky that they had occupied, as well as a part of Tennessee. More important, however, was that the loss of the two forts marked the beginning of a division of the Confederation into two parts.

General Beauregard hurried west as Johnston's deputy, and both generals planned a march south to unite their forces at Corinth (Mississippi). Corinth was an important railway junction which had to be defended. The Confederates therefore denuded their garrisons on the Atlantic coast to bring Johnston's army up to 50,000 men, opposed to the 20,000 men that the U.S. Generals Halleck and Buell then had at their disposal in the west.

The Union now took their time over a further advance. Grant moved with 45,000 men along the Tennessee, while Buell mustering some 25,000 advanced towards Nashville. Grant demanded that the already beaten enemy should be pursued and kept under pressure, but Halleck, who was by then the senior commander in the West, was not impressed and took no notice of his counsel.

The Battle of Shiloh 6.4.–7.4.1862. On account of these delays, the Confederates succeeded in regrouping and reorganizing at Corinth. Grant's army had pitched their camp on the banks of the Tennessee below Savannah, near a place called Pittsburgh Landing Stage. This was only some 23 miles from Corinth. The centre of the army lay near a meeting house known as Shiloh Church.

General Johnston foresaw the danger that Grant would soon oppose him with superior forces. He   31

A naval battery, with, in the background, Nelson House, Yorktown, that was used as a hospital (July 1862).

therefore attacked on 6 April before Grant could be reinforced by Buell. The Union troops were surprised and almost thrown into the Tennessee River, but the soldiers managed to reform and Buell appeared in the evening. Johnston was killed during the battle.

The following day, the fortune of war favoured the Union. Beauregard retired defeated to Corinth, although he was not pursued.

In the first major battle of the Civil War, both sides suffered heavy casualties. The Union sustained some 13,000 killed and wounded, while the Confederates lost 10,000. The latter's *logement* in West Tennessee was erased.

For the Confederates, however, the period of defeats in the West was not yet at an end. A month before – on 6 March 1862 – Major-General Samuel Curtis had defeated the Southern army of Major-General Earl van Dorn in Arkansas.

Gun-boats supported the operations of the army under Brigadier-General John Pope in capturing New Madrid and Island No. 10 in the Mississippi on 7 April.

General Halleck then advanced on Corinth with more than 100,000 men, but General Beauregard did not trust himself to offer battle, as he had less than 50,000 men available. Halleck's advance was extremely cautious and in spite of his superior forces he took no risks. Beauregard, however, was forced to abandon Corinth on 29 and 30 May, and to withdraw into Mississippi.

On 6 June, the Confederate river defence flotilla was decisively beaten on the Mississippi at Memphis.

Further fighting in Virginia. It seemed that in the West, the Union would soon occupy the whole of the Mississippi valley.

On the other hand, their situation in the Virginian theatre was not so favourable. General McClellan was not only too cautious, but his operations were being perpetually criticized by Washington. Finally, he was relieved as Commander-in-Chief in March 1862, although he retained his command of the Potomac army.

Rather than to attack Richmond by way of Manassas, he planned to transport his army by ship to Form Monroe on the Viginian peninsula, and to advance from there to the Confederate capital. Washington was hardly enthusiastic, as the politicians feared a sudden thrust on the Union capital which would thus have been exposed to attack, although McClellan promised to leave enough troops for its defence behind.

Finally, caution abandoned, seventeen divisions – *circa* 90,000 men – were shipped into Fort Monroe, although the Union vessels did not dare to use the James River, which by that time was controlled by the Confederate Ironclad *Virginia*. The advance began on 4 April 1862, but already on the next day McClellan allowed himself to be deceived in front of Yorktown. There, a line of earthworks had been thrown up by the Confederate Major-General John Bankhead Magruder, which was defended by 15,000 soldiers. By means of movements and a lot of noise, McClellan was tricked into believing that there were far more enemy troops in front of him than was the case. As a result, he hesitated to attack, and settled down to besiege the weak Confederate forces. With a bit more energy and enthusiasm, he might easily have routed his enemy.

An entire month elapsed at Yorktown before McClellan undertook any action, giving the Confederates time to bring in reinforcements. On 4 May, however, General Joe Johnston, commander of the Confederate forces in Virginia, pulled his troops back to Richmond, where they moved into well-built fortifications.

It was well known in Richmond just how worried Washington was about the security of their Northern capital. As a result, a diversionary attack was mounted in the Shenandoah Valley, that runs between the Alleghenies in the west and the Blue Ridge Mountains in the east. Since March 1862, 'Stonewall' Jackson, already proving to be one of the most capable Confederate generals, had been stationed at Winchester with 7,000 infantry, 600 cavalry and 27 guns. If the valley were occupied by the Confederates, then not only Washington, but the whole of the eastern industrial area of the Union was threatened. Additionally, the southern part of the valley was important to the Southerners as a source of supply for foodstuffs.

To counter the threat, the Union moved Major-

Major-General George McClellan was facing Yorktown on 5 April 1862. In spite of his superior numbers, he failed to attack, and instead, prepared for a formal siege. Heavy artillery was ordered such as the heavy mortars shown above.

General Nathanial Prentiss Banks with 15,000 men into the valley, who advanced southwards. But 'Stonewall' Jackson in turn received 8,000 men as reinforcements, to hinder Banks from joining McClellan on the march to Richmond, or from occupying the whole of the Shenandoah Valley.

On 8 May, Jackson attacked the troops under Major-General John Charles Frémont who were advancing from the west, and put them to flight. After that, in a furious fight, he pushed the Union troops at Front Royal away to the north. Banks thus found himself threatened from the rear, and leaving behind quantities of supplies and equipment, had to withdraw to Winchester. There he tried to fight a delaying action, but on 25 May was defeated and had to retreat back over the Potomac. The Southerners took 3,000 prisoners, captured 10,000 33 rifles and enormous quantities of equipment of all descriptions. More than 1,500 Union soldiers were killed.

As a result, War Minister Edwin McMasters Stanton came to the conclusion that the Confederates would invade the northern part of the Union through the Shenandoah Valley. Major-General McDowell, who was based at Fredericksburg, and who should have joined up with McClellan on the Chickahominy River near Richmond, had to immediately detach 20,000 men to stop the Confederate advance.

After his successes, Jackson retired slowly southwards with his enormous booty, to Winchester and Strasburg. Both Union generals missed the opportunity to wear him out with flank attacks, and by 5 June, he had reached Harrisburg in the south. On 8 June there was the battle at Cross Keys, where in spite of numerical superiority, the Union was again defeated, and the next day they were once more put to flight at Port Republic. Finally the Confederates marched back to Richmond. Jackson had performed his mission brilliantly, and the Shenandoah campaign will always be remembered by military historians. With less than 18,000 men, between 30 April and 9 June, Jackson had stopped and defeated some 70,000 Union troops. His campaign hindered the Union plan to capture Richmond and thus finish off the war at one stroke.

Union artillery at Fair Oaks Station, where the Confederates under Joseph E. Johnston attacked on 31 May 1862 at the start of the Seven Day Battle. This engagement forced Major-General McClellan to withdraw from Richmond.

McClellan's army in front of Richmond was divided by the Chickahominy, and the Confederates recognized this as a chance to defeat his forces in detail. Although they only had 62,000 men as opposed to 100,000 of the Union, they decided to take the offensive. They had to beat McClellan before he could be reinforced by McDowell, otherwise they would be forced to abandon Richmond.

On 31 May, the Confederates under Joe Johnston attacked the Union left flank at Fair Oaks, but they lacked the necessary experience. On the same evening, Johnston was severely wounded as he tried personally to save the situation. The next day, the Union rallied, forcing the Confederates to abandon the attack. The former lost some 5,000 men in the battle, while the casualties of the latter were *circa* 6,100.

The wounding of Johnston was a heavy blow for the South, and as a result, President Jefferson Davis transferred the command of the Army of Northern Virginia on 1 June to General Robert Edward Lee. With this appointment, one of the greatest generals of all time stepped into the annals of military history.

Robert E. Lee was born on 19 January 1807 in Stratford, Virginia. He entered the West Point Military Academy in 1825, and passed out in 1829 as second-best in his class. After that he served in the Engineer Corps, and took part as a Captain in the Mexican war, where he was decorated. His next appointment was as Commandant of West Point, from 1852 to 1855. Married to a great-great-granddaughter of George Washington, he spent most of his time in Virginia as a typical southern gentleman. In 1855 he was lieutenant-colonel of the 2nd Cavalry Regiment, and when in 1859 John Brown undertook his raid on Harpers Ferry, he was suppressed by Lee.

Although Lee was a member of the southern aristocracy, he had no sympathy with the secessionist movement – he had even liberated his slaves.

At the outset of the war, Lincoln offered him on 18 April 1861 the command of the Union troops. When, however, Virginia, his home state, left the Union, Colonel Robert E. Lee declined the offer on 20 April and handed in his resignation.

In the rank of general, Lee tried without success to drive the Union out of West Virginia in September

General Robert Edward Lee (1807–70) was not only the most famous of the Confederate generals in the Civil War, but can also be numbered among the great commanders of history.

1861. Then from November 1861 to March 1862, he was responsible for building fortifications on the Atlantic coast, and afterwards, until the end of May, was President Jefferson Davis's military advisor.

The Seven Day Battle. As soon as 'Stonewall' Jackson arrived back from the Shenandoah campaign, the new commander of the Army of North Virginia went over to the offensive. Robert E. Lee had roughly 90,000 men at his disposal.

The Seven Day Battle began on 26 June at Mechanicsville, where the Union troops found themselves in an unfavourable position. Some 30,000 men lay north of the Chickahominy and 60,000 to the south of this small river.

The Union withstood the Southern attack, because Lee's plan was frustrated by the inexperience of both officers and troops. They were, however, forced to retire to Gaine's Mill on account of the firm pressure.

On 27 June, 65,000 Confederate troops opposed the Union army, that in a series of rearguard actions withdrew south over the Chickahominy.

U.S. Navy warships with an observation balloon on the James River.

McClellan let himself be fooled into believing that Lee's main attack would be made in the north, and not in the south, although it was pointed out to him that in the south he had the chance to advance directly on Richmond, without meeting serious resistance. He stuck to his own opinion, however, and ordered the Potomac Army to retire south to the James River, and there, supported by gun-boats, to build new defensive positions. Lee realized at once that McClellan had given up the idea of capturing Richmond, and did everything within his power to hinder the Union withdrawal to the James River.

There was another battle at Savage's Station, but the Union line held firm, and in further actions at Frayser's Farm and Glendale on 30 June, the Southerners were equally unable to defeat the Northerners.

On 1 July, Lee attacked the Union army at Malvern Hill on the James River, but was beaten off by the well-placed enemy artillery, with the loss of some 5,000 men. Malvern Hill was a local Union victory, but McClellan, who had stationed himself in a gun-boat on the river, ordered his victorious troops to withdraw to Harrison's Landing.

On 30 July 1862, the Confederates commanded by General Robert E. Lee attacked the Union forces at Glendale and Frayser's Farm, in an attempt to push them into the marshes of White Oak Swamp.

Thus the Seven Day Battle was ended. The Union had readily thrown back the Confederate attacks, but McClellan was obsessed with the feeling that he would be defeated and forced to withdraw. He let slip a golden opportunity, and with a bit more courage and decisiveness could have taken Richmond.

The casualties on both sides had their own tale to tell. The Union lost 1,734 killed, 8,062 wounded and some 6,000 prisoners, while the Confederates suffered 3,487 dead, 16,261 wounded and 875 prisoners.

Although the Yankees had not been beaten, and the morale of the Potomac army remained high in spite of the perpetual retreats, the Rebs could justly claim a victory. General Lee had succeeded in driving the enemy away from Richmond.

Without the help of the heavy and accurate fire of the gun-boats of the Navy, McClellan would not have been able to withdraw to Harrison's Landing.

The victory had important results as far as the South was concerned. The inexperienced Confederate troops had learnt much during the seven days, and after these battles regarded themselves as veterans. Robert E. Lee got to know his generals and from then on was able to estimate their capabilities. All regarded him as a gallant, clever and imaginative officer, who for the first time had had the opportunity to demonstrate his strategic and tactical capabilities. Right up to the end of the war, he remained undefeated.

The South realized that General Robert E. Lee was the victor and that they should seize the initiative. Under Lee, the political and military situation of the Confederacy reached its peak in the following months.

Now the first indications of the isolation of the South through Northern sea power were, however, becoming apparent.

A Union field hospital at Savage Station on 30 June 1862, at the end of the Seven Day Battle.

The War on the Rivers and at Sea

Preceding pages. The last major battle on the Western rivers took place on the Mississippi on 6 June 1862. Using five powerful Ironclads and four ram-ships, Commodore Charles Davis defeated eight Confederate vessels commanded by Captain James Montgomery – hardly a Confederate ship escaped. The photograph overleaf shows the U.S.S. Cairo.

The war at sea. In the struggles on the great rivers of North America, off the coasts and on the high seas, it was not the purpose of the Union to provoke great naval battles. Their plan was to cut off the Confederacy from sea-borne supplies, and thus paralyse her economy. This in turn would, it was hoped, destroy the enemy's will to continue the war.

On the outbreak of hostilities, the Union had no particular concept of maritime strategy, and was totally unprepared for the tasks that lay ahead. Like most other fleets, the U.S. Navy was in a state of transition from sailing ships to steamers.

In 1862 the Union had ninety ships of all classes available, but only forty-two vessels were in commission, twenty-one of which were regarded as obsolete. In March 1862, the fleet was stationed as follows: twelve ships formed the home squadron, four units lay in the northern harbours and the rest had to be brought back from their overseas stations.

The ships had been designed for work on the high seas, and not for use in the narrow and dangerous coastal waters or on the inland rivers. It was first necessary to adapt to this latter type of warfare.

When the war started, the Confederacy possessed scarcely any warships ready for service. As early as 21 February 1861, President Jefferson Davis appointed as minister in charge of the Confederate States Navy Stephen Russell Mallory, who immediately got down to the seemingly insoluble problem of building up a navy from scratch.

Mallory had plenty of experience of shipping, as he had been Chairman of the Senate Naval Affairs Committee since 1853, whereby he had been involved in modernizing the Federal navy.

Some 200 regular naval officers placed themselves at the disposal of the Confederacy, which simplified

Stephen Russell Mallory, the Confederate Navy Minister, built up a fleet from scratch in spite of insurmountable difficulties.

Mallory's task to a certain extent. The problem was that at the outset they only possessed twelve ships, such as customs cutters and merchant vessels that they had confiscated. Additionally, the Southern States lacked experienced and trained crews, as prior to 1861, exports had been handled by Northern shippers. Thus it was hardly to be wondered at that the North showed far more understanding of naval matters.

During the course of the war, the South made a virtue out of necessity, although the disadvantages could not be overcome on account of the economic and industrial situation. As opposed to the U.S. Navy, which contributed little to the development of new ship types and weapon systems, with the exception of the monitors, the South first sent ships known as Ironclads into battle. They discovered mines that could be electrically detonated under water (known as torpedoes), and built the world's first submarine that succeeded in sinking an enemy ship. Additionally they fitted warships with rams, that had fallen into disuse during the development of large sailing ships, and Confederate steamers cruised on all the oceans of the world, inflicting immeasurable damage to the Northern merchant marine.

In the end, however, the Confederacy, as on land, succumbed at sea to the superiority of the Union. They were not only inferior in strength to the North, but lacked also adequate coastal facilities. The lengthy southern coastline had innumerable bays, river mouths and deltas which could only be reached by shallow-draught ships. Only ten harbours had a railway connexion with the interior, and only six of these, Wilmington, Charleston, Savannah, Pensacola, Mobile and New Orleans, had through connexions with other States. Norfolk was the only harbour that could be used by deep-draught vessels, and only there, and at Pensacola and New Orleans, were there ship-building facilities.

The first sea engagements. As soon as one of the Southern states left the Union, the Union's ships and establishments were immediately requisitioned. At the inauguration of President Lincoln on 4 March 1861, only Fort Sumter in Charleston Harbor and Fort Pickens at the entrance to Pensacola (Florida) were still occupied by the North. South Carolina left the Union on 20 December 1860, and the Northern flag flying from Fort Sumter was regarded as being 'foreign', so that the tension be-

tween both sides became daily more explosive. After lengthy consideration, President Lincoln decided to support Fort Sumter with warships, and on 4 April issued the necessary orders. On the same day, the new Union Navy Minister, Gideon Welles, gave instructions for the warships *Powhatan*, *Pawnee*, *Pocohontas* and the customs cutter *Harriet Lane* to relieve the fort, using force if required.

Gideon Welles, born in 1802 at Glastenburg/Connecticut, studied law and entered politics at an early age. He was regarded as an anti-slavery democrat and was a member of the Republican party. Although relatively inexperienced in naval matters, he created a powerful navy during the course of the war, that played an important part in the final defeat of the South.

On 12 April, the Union ships were near the fort, but on the same day the Confederate batteries opened fire, an event which signified the beginning of the Civil War. The warships did not join the fighting, and after the surrender, they took the garrison under Major Robert Anderson on board, and returned to New York.

A blockade runner struggles to reach shelter in harbour.

On 17 April 1861, President Jefferson Davis appealed to all Southern ship owners to apply to have letters of marque issued to them, in order to destroy Northern shipping on the high seas. The reason for this step was that the Confederation still did not have any armed ships available. They believed that by introducing privateers and thus interrupting commercial shipping, the European countries would be brought in on their side. In addition, it was hoped that the privateers (and later the auxiliary cruisers) would force the Union to lift their blockade of the Southern states.

As a result, President Lincoln announced the blockade of *all* the States from South Carolina to Texas which had left the Union. By imposing a total blockade, however, the Union committed a blunder, as according to international law, they could only close the harbours of the Southern states – they were dealing with States which had left the Union, not a foreign power. Thus there was the danger that other countries would recognize the Confederacy, and England and France did not hesitate to grant belligerent's rights.

At that time, however, neither side was in a position to achieve their aims. The Union had to maintain the blockade, and the Confederacy had either to evade it or prove that it was impractical and only existed on paper.

Navy Minister Mallory did not have any warships to use effectively against Union shipping, although one solution was to buy them abroad. The Confederation, though, right at the outset of hostilities, missed the chance to purchase an efficient fleet from the proceeds of cotton sales, as well as to buy up the ships of the British East India Company, which had handed over the conduct of their affairs to the British crown.

All the foregoing, as well as the embargo on cotton exports that was imposed, demonstrated that Mallory, for all his organizing abilities, had not realized the importance of the impending naval war. He was convinced that only armoured ships would break the blockade and chase off the wooden vessels of the Union. At the beginning of May 1861, James D. Bulloch was sent to England to buy warships and to try to get a *Gloire* class frigate from France.

Commander James Dunwoody Bulloch represented the Confederate navy in England where he organized the building and equipping of auxiliary cruisers. The navy had reason to be grateful for his experience and diplomatic talent.

from the Union on 17 April 1861 posed a special threat to the important naval base at Norfolk. There lay, among other ships, the steam frigate *Merrimac* of 3,200 tons and armed with forty guns, that was undergoing repairs. Because of the tense situation, everything possible was done to move the five-year-old ship to Philadelphia. The yard commandant and his workmen, who sympathized with the South, did their best to delay the departure of the vessel.

Navy Minister Welles did everything in his power to see that neither ships nor the heavy guns and munitions stored in the arsenal would fall into the hands of the South. The U.S. navy officers on the spot were convinced that the shipyard could not be defended, and thus the evacuation was begun on 20 April. Nine warships were set on fire and sank in the harbour. Only the *Pawnee* and the *Cumberland* got away, being brought out by a tug during the night of the 21st. A number of the warships only sank though to the waterline, among them the *Merrimac*.

On account of this hasty action, the South obtained a large quantity of guns and *matériel* that was

42 **The evacuation of Norfolk.** The secession of Virginia

urgently required. They gained more than 1,000 guns, as well as 2,000 barrels of powder, but even more important was the fact that the dry-dock remained undamaged, so that large ships could be repaired.

The blockade. In the meanwhile, Union warships strengthened the announced blockade. Initially only three ships were available, but Navy Minister Welles bought up hundreds of vessels in order to achieve his aim of strangling the South economically. The blockade, nevertheless, posed problems, in that the Union did not have a harbour on the southern coast where they could overhaul their ships or take on coal and supplies. It was therefore decided to capture a number of harbours as well as to divide the blockading forces into two squadrons, in order to simplify their assigned tasks.

The importance of the Mississippi. This mighty river divided the Confederacy into two halves. The control of this strategically important waterway was vital for the North, in that they could isolate the Southern states from the West. The Union immediately purchased three wooden paddle steamers to be converted into gun-boats, and protected them from bombardment by fitting heavy outer planking. As early as 9 September these vessels were ready for service and operating successfully on the Mississippi. The most important units of the Union forces already on the river were seven armoured gun-boats, the *Cairo*, *Carondelet*, *Cincinnati*, *Mound City*, *St. Louis*, *Louisville* and *Pittsburgh*. Captain Andrew H. Foote took command of this powerful fleet on 5 September 1861.

At the end of the following January the Ironclads were serviced for active service, and they were later joined by a number of schooners armed with powerful mortars.

Confederate privateers and auxiliary cruisers. In the meanwhile, on 18 May, the schooner *Savannah* was the first Confederate vessel to be issued with letters of marque. That signified the beginning of one of the legendary epochs of the Civil War.

The main privateer bases were Charleston and New Orleans. In the early months such vessels were able to notch up notable successes – the famous brig *Jefferson Davis* took nine prizes between June and August 1861. The difficulty was that the Confederates could not sell their prizes profitably. On account of

the blockade they could not bring them into Southern state harbours, and the European powers closed their ports to prizes. Because of this, privateering was abandoned at the end of 1861.

The voyages of the privateers and auxiliary cruisers had far reaching results, however. Panic broke out in the American merchant marine – the second largest after England – when the news of the first seizures arrived. Insurance premiums and freight rates rocketed upwards, so that the British were able to offer far more reasonable terms and with time to monopolize the trade with America. Additionally, the Northerners sold many of their merchant ships to neutrals to avoid further losses, a step from which in 1917 the U.S. merchant marine was still suffering adverse effects on entry to the First World War.

C.S. Auxiliary cruiser *Sumter*. Raphael Semmes was one of the most famous Confederate naval officers and auxiliary cruiser captains. He was born in Piscaraway in Maryland and entered the Navy in 1826. While serving on a number of ships he managed to find time to study law, and with the rank of Commander, he became Secretary on the Lighthouse Board in Washington. Resigning from the Navy on 15 February 1861, on 18 April he was appointed to command the steamer *Habana* that in peace-time had voyaged between Cuba and New Orleans.

Semmes decided to convert the 347-ton screw-driven steamer, which was lying in New Orleans, into an auxiliary cruiser. After two months under his untiring supervision, the rebuild was completed, and on 3 June, she was commissioned as the C.S. auxiliary cruiser *Sumter*.

The armament of the vessel consisted of one 8-in. gun and four 32 pounders. The crew was made up of eleven officers, seventy-two sailors and twenty marines. The break-out from the Mississippi Delta was doubly difficult on account of navigational problems and the close blockade by Union warships. Captain Semmes succeeded, however, in reaching the open sea on 30 June 1861.

His orders were, in the shortest space of time to cause as much damage to the enemy as possible.

As early as 3 July, the U.S. sailing ship *Golden Rocket* fell into the hands of the cruiser, and its fate

The auxiliary cruiser Sumter *approaches a sailing ship. This was the first of the Confederate commerce raiders, and under the command of Commander Semmes, she took a considerable number of prizes between July 1861 and January 1862.*

was sealed when Semmes set it on fire as he could not take his prize back home. This seizure and the appearance of the *Sumter* caused great excitement in the North, and the Navy Minister, Welles, was empowered to hunt the Confederate cruiser with every available ship, even if this meant weakening the blockade. Several warships were sent after the *Sumter* – as well as the other Confederate auxiliary cruisers – but communications were so inadequate in those days that the Union vessels always arrived too late on the scene of events.

On 4 July, to the south of Cuba, the *Sumter* seized two schooners, on the next day two further prizes, and on the 6th, three more, all of which were brought into Cienfuegos. Because of Spanish neutrality, however, all the prizes had to be set free.

The cruiser took on coal in order to continue her operations, and on 7 July left Cienfuegos on a course for north-west Brazil. In spite of some difficulties, it proved possible to restock with coal in

Curaçao, but Semmes had to realize that the Union could cause trouble for Southern state ships in all the harbours of the world.

On 27 July, the *Sumter* seized the schooner *Abbey Bradford*, which was sent off with a prize crew to try to reach a Southern port, but she fell into the hands of the U.S.S. *Powhatan* on 13 August.

In the meanwhile, Semmes had put into Port of Spain in Trinidad on 4 August and on the following day left for Brazil, taking in coal at Cayenne and Paramaribo on the way.

During the voyage, two more ships were seized but as the *Sumter* lay in St. Pierre on Martinique, the U.S. cruiser *Iroquois* appeared on the scene, but Semmes was able to give her the slip.

By that time, his ship had to be overhauled, and Semmes decided to sail to France. On the way three further ships were burnt and one allowed to go free. On 3 January, the cruiser anchored at Cadiz in Spain, but as the Spanish authorities made difficulties and several crew members deserted, she moved on to Gibraltar. In the Straits, the *Sumter* destroyed her last ship, although she had to let another one go free.

Commander Semmes saw no possibility of overhauling his ship in Gibraltar, besides which three U.S. cruisers were waiting outside to bombard her to pieces. He therefore suggested that the vessel should either be laid up or sold. On 7 April he received orders to abandon her and to return home.

As a result of his successes, he had in the meanwhile been promoted to captain.

The Union breathed a sigh of relief when it was heard that the first Confederate cruiser had been rendered inactive, even though their own warships could not claim the credit. During her period of active service, the *Sumter* had seized eighteen ships, seven of which had been burnt.

The capture of naval bases. The Confederate blockade runners made great use of Hatteras Inlet (North Carolina), a main channel into the Pamlico Sound. The inlet was strategically important for the Union, so that they decided to occupy it as swiftly as possible.

On 13 August 1861, Brigadier-General Thomas John Wood was ordered to capture Hatteras Inlet, together with Flag-Officer Silas Horton Stringham, the naval officer in charge of the landing. On 28 August, the warships opened fire on Forts Hatteras and Clark, and a short while afterwards the troops were put ashore. The next afternoon, both forts surrendered, providing the Union with their first naval base in the South where their blockading vessels could take on coal and supplies.

On 29 October, the largest fleet that up until then had been seen, comprising seventy-seven warships, left Fort Monroe with 16,000 troops on board, all under the command of Flag-Officer Samuel Francis du Pont. Its target was Port Royal in South Carolina, and the Confederates were not in a position to oppose this mass of troops and *matériel* with anything approaching equal numbers. On 7 November the forts protecting the entrance to Port Royal were bombarded, and surrendered the same day. As a result, the Union gun-boats were able to command the coastline between Savannah and Charleston, although on their voyages they ran up against mines (known then as torpedoes) for the first time.

The Union's next aim was to effect a landing on Roanoke Island to the north of Hatteras Inlet. Commanded by Flag-Officer L. M. Goldsborough, the Union warships left Hampton Roads (Fort Monroe) on 12 January 1862, and on 7 February they commenced the bombardment. The troops were landed in the afternoon after the fort had been neutralized and the island was occupied the following day. This meant that Norfolk was isolated, and the gun-boats could control the Albemarle Sound – with the result that three months later the Confederates evacuated what had been their main naval base.

Supported by warships, Northern troops occupied all the harbours in North Carolina, leaving the Confederacy with only two ports on the Atlantic – Charleston and Wilmington – both of which were vitally important for the blockade runners.

In a comparatively short space of time, the Union navy had achieved far-reaching successes, in spite of the defeats suffered by their armies on land.

U.S.S. *Monitor* and C.S.S. *Virginia*. With the construction of these two ships and the ensuing battle between them, the era of the wooden warship finally came to an end, although throughout the Civil War, the latter still had to bear the brunt of the struggle. The so-called monitors were intended for use on rivers and in shallow coastal waters – they proved impractical on the high seas.

The idea of an armoured ship was not a new one at the time. Both England and France had similar vessels, the *Warrior* and the *Gloire*. During the Civil War, the South started constructing armoured ships, the first one being the *Manassas*, originally a screw-driven steamer, that was strengthened with iron plates and wooden planks. The deck had a convex shape so that the ship looked like a floating cigar.

On 12 October 1861, the *Manassas*, in company with two other vessels, attacked the Union warships lying near the mouth of the Mississippi and damaged two of them.

Both the Union and the Confederacy had realized the importance of armoured ships at about the same time. On 3 August 1861, Navy Minister Welles was empowered to establish a committee of three experienced naval officers, to examine plans for building armoured steamships. As early as 16 September they recommended the construction of three vessels, the *Galena*, *New Ironsides* and *Monitor*.

Only the latter was destined to become famous. Her designer, John Ericsson, had to struggle with appalling difficulties before the model that he presented was accepted. When he finally was awarded the contract, it was conditional on his delivering the ship within a hundred days. The keel was laid on 25 October 1861 at the Continental Iron Works yard at Greenpoint (New York), and on 30 January 1862 she was launched. The next day the boiler was already under steam, and on 19 February she was moved to the Brooklyn Navy Yard to be fitted out with her armament and ancillary equipment. At the same time, she made her first test runs. There were great difficulties in fitting the two 11-in. muzzle loading guns into the turret, as this proved to be too small. Thus it initially had to do without a roof, although railway lines were later introduced.

Lieutenant John Lorimer was appointed captain of the *Monitor*, which was commissioned on 25 February. On 6 March she set sail on a course for Hampton Roads, where three days later, the famous combat with the C.S.S. *Virginia* took place.

Confederate attempts to buy Ironclads abroad both then and in the future were unsuccessful. On 30 May 1861, however, the steam frigate *Merrimac* which

The first Civil War Ironclad was the Manassas *which attacked the U.S. warships in the Head of the Passes on 12 October 1861. On 24 April 1862, the Ironclad fired on the Union warships that were trying to run past Forts Jackson and St. Philippe on the Mississippi. During the engagement, she was damaged and exploded.*

had been sunk at Norfolk, was raised; Lieutenant John M. Brooke producing a plan for an armoured ship, which was used by the naval constructor Lieutenant John L. Porter as a basis for his ideas. The result was the *Virginia*, which had sloping armoured sides, and the bow and stern under water. On 11 July 1861, an order was issued for the *Merrimac* to be reconstructed according to the latter design, and to be made ready for service.

As a result, both the Confederacy and the Union were building an armoured vessel at roughly the same time, so that a competition was created as to who would be finished first, and thus able to threaten their opponent.

Work was in progress day and night on the *Virginia*, until she could be commissioned by Captain Franklin S. Buchanan on 17 February 1862.

Captain Franklin Buchanan (1800–74) commanded the Virginia *during the engagement at Hampton Roads. As Admiral, he was forced to lower his flag in surrender from the Ironclad* Tennessee *during the battle in Mobile Bay on 5 August 1864.*

In order to be able more easily to understand the battle between the two Ironclads, the following is a data comparison of the vessels. In contrast to her opponent, the *Virginia* was a monster, too slow and difficult to manoeuvre – she looked like a floating house-roof. She was some 273 feet long and her beam was *circa* 40 feet. The 'roof' was constructed from 20-in. pine logs, on top of which was a layer of 4-in.-thick oak planks, armoured with 2-in. iron plates. The sides fell at an angle of 45 deg. and extended some 8½ inches over the gun deck. The armament consisted of a 6·75-in. gun in the 'gable', with on each side one 6-in. rifled gun and three 8·8-in. smooth bores. (The original *Merrimac* displaced 3,200 tons.)

In contrast, the *Monitor* with her displacement of only 987 tons looked extremely small – like a cheese box on a raft. Mounted in the middle of the deck was only the rotatable turret with a diameter of *circa* 6¼ feet. The wheelhouse was at the front, just over 3

feet high and made from iron bars. Before going into action, the funnel was folded down.

Both Ironclads suffered from severe disadvantages. The *Virginia*'s ram was not properly fixed and proved to be a great hindrance. The rudder and the propeller were insufficiently protected, and the engine could not produce enough power for more than about 5 knots.

The Achilles heel of the *Monitor* was the wheelhouse, as the helmsman could easily be put out of action with one shot. He sat on a platform inside the hull and his head and shoulders projected into the wheelhouse, the only vision being provided by a 1-in.-wide slit. The connexion between the captain and the gunnery officer was poorly organized – a speaking tube on the floor only opened when the turret was in the fore and aft position. A wheel and an iron bar coupled with a machine was used to turn the turret. This operation was so complicated, however, that it was extremely difficult to rotate and could only be stopped with great effort.

The *Virginia*'s greatest disadvantage was her draught of 20 feet, so that she was unsuitable both for use in shallow coastal waters as well as for operations on the open sea.

Captain Buchanan planned to appear at Newport News on 7 March together with five smaller warships. The U.S. frigates *Congress* and *Cumberland* were anchored there, but on account of bad weather, Buchanan could only execute his plan on the following day. In spite of the fact that the *Virginia* had not yet been tested and the crew was untrained, the captain was prepared to take the risk.

The North was aware that the *Virginia* could appear at any moment, so that there was a certain amount of unease among the ships in Hampton Roads. On the morning of 8 March, the frigate *Cumberland* (1,726 tons and fifty guns) was anchored at Newport News Point, and somewhat further away lay the *Congress* (1,867 tons and fifty guns). Near Fort Monroe lay the *Roanoke* (forty-six guns), the *Minnesota* (forty-six guns) and the sailing frigate *St. Lawrence* (fifty-two guns), as well as six gun-boats and several transport and supply ships.

At around 9 a.m., a ship lying at anchor in the James River had been observed from on board the 47

Cumberland, but all remained quiet until mid-day. At 12.40 a.m., the *Mount Vernon* signalled that the enemy vessel was approaching, but the Union blockade ships took no notice until the former fired a gun. In the meanwhile, the *Virginia* had rounded Craney Island at the mouth of the James River. Too late the *Minnesota, Roanoke* and *St. Lawrence* rushed to assist the frigates *Congress* and *Cumberland*, running aground in the process.

Buchanan's main aim was to eliminate the *Cumberland*, which had rifled guns. At 14.10 hours, the *Congress* opened fire on the approaching monster, but the shots bounced harmlessly off. Then in her turn, the *Virginia* turned her guns on the *Congress*, and in a short time shot her to pieces. She then rammed the *Cumberland* twice, which quickly sank, and fired again at the grounded *Congress*. All the while the shore batteries were trying to put the Confederate vessel out of action, but even direct hits did little damage – the armour plating proved itself. The *Virginia* then sank a transporter and a schooner, before turning her attention again to the *Congress*, in the narrow waters. The latter hoisted a white flag to signify surrender, and Confederate sailors boarded the Union warship. At that moment, however, the *Virginia* was bombarded so mightily from all sides – even from the *Congress* herself – that Captain Buchanan fired incendiary shells at the frigate, which finally exploded at around midnight. Under cover of the darkness, the Ironclad withdrew. There was great triumph in the Southern states over the success of the engagement, which had demonstrated that from then on, wooden warships no longer stood a chance against armoured vessels.

The *Monitor* left New York on 6 March en route for Hampton Roads, although on the way she ran into a heavy storm and nearly foundered. On 8 March she anchored at 9 o'clock in the evening in the vicinity of the frigate *Roanoke*, but moved later to protect the *Minnesota* from attack by the *Virginia*.

At about 6 o'clock in the morning on the following day, the Confederate Ironclad reappeared in Hampton Roads, to try to sink the remaining Union ships. The *Minnesota* signalled to the *Monitor* to move up. Lieutenant Worden had prepared a plan of action whereby he intended to circle around the enemy and to destroy her with fire at point blank

The struggle between the Monitor *and the* Virginia *in Hampton Roads on 9 March 1862.*

range from his 11-in. guns. The shots from both ships bounced harmlessly off each other's armour plate, however, and the scene of action was hidden by dense clouds of powder smoke. *Virginia* tried without success to ram the *Monitor*. In this engagement, the *Monitor* had the great advantage that, except for the turret, she was an extremely difficult target to hit. When *Virginia* ran aground during a turning manoeuvre, Lieutenant Worden closed in for the kill, intending to finally destroy the monster. As it happened, the shells possessed by both ships did not achieve the desired effect. It later became apparent that the powder filling in the *Monitor*'s shells was far too weak, while the steel shells for the *Virginia* had been left behind in Norfolk.

As the *Monitor* then turned away, her opponent fired a shell from her stern gun right into the wheelhouse and wounded the captain. Lieutenant Green then took command, and steered into shallow waters where he could not be followed by the *Virginia*. The latter finally struggled free and withdrew to Norfolk to take on fresh ammunition and inspect the damage sustained, as it was intended to renew the conflict as soon as possible. The damage was more serious than had been expected; the bow had been damaged where the ram had been torn off, with the result that the *Virginia* was taking in water. Even some of the iron plates had been torn by the impact of shells from her opponent. Other than on the wheelhouse, the latter was hardly damaged, except that the turret was well dented.

The first battle between Ironclads had been fought, and the days of the sail warship were finally over. During the following weeks the *Monitor* was not permitted to renew the struggle with the *Virginia*, as she was the only armoured ship that the Union possessed, and could not under any circumstances be risked at sea. Further vessels of the same type were not yet ready, but after the fight in Hampton Roads, the U.S. Navy placed orders for further types armed with 15-in. guns.

Engagements on the Mississippi. The next target for the Ironclads on the Mississippi was Island No. 10, just below the point where the Ohio flows into the main river. On 14 March 1862, seven gun-boats and ten bomb-vessels left their base at Cairo, to open fire on the island. The bombardment started on 16 March, but the struggle lasted for several weeks without success for the Union. Finally, first one and

then the other Ironclads ran past the island, to attack it from the rear. The Confederate garrison surrendered on 7 April, with the result that the upper Mississippi was lost as far as the Southern states were concerned.

South of Island No. 10 was the powerful Fort Pillow, which the Union army and gun-boat fleet also wished to neutralize. On 10 May, however, the Confederate River Defence Fleet attacked the Union Ironclads in an effort to drive them off. The U.S. Ironclad *Cincinnati* was rammed and sunk, while the *Mound City* ran aground. As a result of experience gained in this engagement, the gun-boats were further reinforced with railway lines, in order to be able to cope quickly with any sort of attack.

During the following weeks, the army under General Grant increased their pressure on the fort to such an extent that it had to be evacuated on 4 and 5 June. The warships, which had been commanded by Captain Charles H. Davis since 9 May, then steamed to Memphis, where a battle took place on 6 June. Five Union gun-boats and two ram-ships attacked the Confederate River Defence Fleet, under Captain Montgomery, and totally destroyed it, with the result that Memphis capitulated without a fight. Thus the way to Vicksburg was free, the Confederates' most strategically important point on the Mississippi.

The capture of New Orleans. The North had been planning for quite some time to recapture this important city at the mouth of the Mississippi, from the Confederates, whereby the latter would lose their last major harbour for the use of their blockade runners. Only the U.S. Navy could put this plan into effect. Firstly, the Forts St. Philip and Jackson which commanded the channel through the Mississippi Delta to New Orleans had to be neutralized. For this mission it was proposed to use bomb-schooners, fitted with 12-in. mortars, and commanded by Lieutenant David D. Porter. The overall commander of the fleet was Captain David Glasgow Farragut, who had been working on the necessary plans to break through and capture the city, since February 1862. The Union warships assembled at the Head of Passes in the Mississippi Delta.

On 18 April, Porter began a five-day bombardment 49

David Glasgow Farragut (1801–70), the victor of New Orleans and Mobile Bay. In 1862 he was promoted to Rear-Admiral, in 1864 to Vice-Admiral and 1866 to Admiral of the U.S. Navy.

cruiser *Hartford*, ran aground, but managed to free herself.

Several Confederate warships were destroyed, including the *Manassas*, which sank. Two hours later, Farragut had succeeded in getting past the forts, and on the following day he appeared in front of New Orleans, which surrendered. The two forts held out until 28 April, when they too surrendered, and on 1 May, the city was occupied by the army. On the same day, the Ironclad *Louisiana* blew up, as she had been abandoned by her crew.

Captain Farragut steamed on up the river, but he did not succeed in capturing Vicksburg. He soon returned downstream, as there was a risk that his ships would remain isolated there if the water level dropped.

David Dixon Porter (1813–91) commanded the Union fleet and was Grant's deputy at the capture of Vicksburg. He succeeded his step-brother Farragut as Admiral of the U.S. Navy in 1870.

of the forts with twenty bomb-schooners, but without achieving any notable success. Captain Farragut decided, therefore, to use his seventeen ships, armed with a total of 154 guns, to run past the forts at night and thus to break through to the city. The Confederate side took the necessary defensive measures. The Ironclad *Louisiana*, commanded by Commander John K. Mitchell and with shipyard workers on board, steamed from New Orleans to the forts. As further reinforcements, the Ironclad gun-boat *Manassas*, two armed steamers and four smaller gun-boats were despatched.

At 2 o'clock in the morning of 24 April, Captain Farragut gave the signal for the breakthrough. Six armoured gun-boats and two sloops led the flotilla.

50 In the following artillery duel, the flagship, the

One of the schooners armed with mortars that formed part of the Union flotilla commanded by David D. Porter that bombarded Forts Jackson and St. Philippe to the south of New Orleans on 18 April 1862.

With immense difficulty, the Confederates had made ready the Ironclad *Arkansas*, armed with ten guns. Lieutenant Isaac N. Brown took her out, and on 15 July encountered the U.S. Ironclad *Carondelet*, the gun-boat *Taylor* and the ram-ship *Queen of the West*, all of which were damaged in the subsequent engagement. In spite of Farragut's fleet, the *Arkansas* managed to reach Vicksburg, much to the surprise of the besieged town, and all the Union efforts to put her out of action failed.

Farragut withdrew to Baton Rouge on 24 July, where he was attacked by the Confederates, supported by the *Arkansas*. The latter ship, however, on account of engine damage, was not fully operative, and on the following day she was hit so badly that her commander, Lieutenant Henry Stevens, had to blow her up. David Glasgow Farragut was promoted to Rear-Admiral on 16 June, the first U.S. navy officer to hold that rank.

On 30 September, the U.S. warships on the Mississippi, which had previously operated under the overall command of the Army, became the Mississippi squadron. From then on they were controlled by the Navy, and their commander was Rear-Admiral David Dixon Porter.

The Triumph of the South

Confederate victories. The U.S. Navy had won not only tactical, but also important although not immediately apparent strategic successes, but at the same time, the Confederacy on land reached the peak of its military glory. It seemed in the summer of 1862, through its offensive in the North, that the Confederacy was near to total victory over the Union. The reasons for this were that the Southern troops were brilliantly led, while the Union armies were more or less in the hands of incompetents. For a long time the North had no overall Commander-in-Chief, until they finally picked on Major-General Harry Wager Halleck, who had previously been successful in the West. He had driven the Confederates out of Kentucky and Missouri, and captured the western part of Tennessee.

General Halleck (born in 1815) had, like many other officers, studied at West Point, where he passed out as third best of his class. He occupied himself with

Major-General Henry Wager Halleck (1815–72) from whom, initially, President Lincoln expected great things. Halleck had little energy and no strategic or tactical talent, although he was appointed as Commander-in-Chief of all the Union armies on 11 July 1862. He was not always in full control, but possessed excellent administrative talents. In March 1864 he was replaced by Grant, but remained until the end of the war as Chief-of-Staff.

military science quite early in his career, and had written several books. Leaving the Army in 1854, as a captain, he studied law. In August 1861, President Lincoln recalled him from retirement and promoted him to major-general. In the early campaigns in the West, he proved to be a capable organizer and administrator, but Halleck never possessed the talent to lead the large Civil War armies in the field.

His initial task was to stop any further calamities. McClellan still lay on the James River, and could easily have taken the offensive with a chance of capturing Richmond. In North Virginia there was a new Union army of some 50,000 men (the Army of Virginia), which had been commanded by Brigadier-General John Pope since 26 June 1862. Pope had made his name in the actions which had resulted in the capture of New Madrid and Island No. 10 on the Mississippi. His troops now marched along the Orange and Alexandria Railroad, from Gordonsville in the direction of Richmond. At the same time he had to cover Washington and close off the north of the Shenandoah Valley. The Union imagined that General Lee would find it impossible to deal with both their armies at the same time.

General Robert E. Lee, however, had the ability to judge his enemies correctly. He therefore remained with the bulk of his Army in front of Richmond, as he knew that McClellan was a ditherer, and sent General 'Stonewall' Jackson to the north to attack Pope.

General Halleck recognized the danger that if his two armies did not get moving, their numerical superiority would avail them little. They would be defeated in detail by the far more energetic Confederate generals.

McClellan could not be persuaded, however, to advance on Richmond, as he clung to the opinion that the enemy was far superior to his forces, and the desired reinforcements were being witheld by Washington.

On 3 August, therefore, President Lincoln ordered the Potomac Army to be transported back to Washington by sea.

Lee seized the opportunity to attack Pope. At all costs, Jackson wanted to hinder the latter from crossing the Rappahannock River, and on 9 August, to the west of Cedar Mountain, he came up against advance detachments of Union cavalry. The engagement developed into a battle, which it seemed that the Union would win, but towards evening the Confederates drove the enemy back towards Culpeper. Pope then advanced against Jackson, who had to realize that he no longer had a chance to defeat the Virginia Army in detail.

Pope's army was more of a threat to the Confederates than they had imagined, especially in view of the fact that he could be reinforced by McClellan. It was this that Lee had to hinder, and leaving only 20,000 men behind at Richmond, he marched his army to Gordonsville, where he arrived on 15 August. Together with Jackson he thus had some 55,000 men on strength.

Second Battle of Bull Run or Manassas. General Robert E. Lee has often been criticized for his handling of the following operations, as he divided his force into two corps, which, according to the military textbooks, one should not do when faced by the enemy. Brigadier-General James Longstreet commanded Corps I, or the right wing, and 'Stonewall' Jackson Corps II, or the left wing. On 19 August, Pope had withdrawn across the Rappahannock to avoid being encircled in the east by the Confederates. Lee, however, had to act swiftly, as he had received intelligence of the approach of reinforcements from McClellan to the tune of two corps. His plan was for Longstreet to occupy the Union troops on the Rappahannock,

During the brilliant encircling manoeuvre of 25–26 August 1862, before the second Battle of Bull Run or Manassas, Jackson's troops destroyed a section of the Orange and Alexandria Railroad. In the photograph on pages 52–3, Union engineers are repairing a bridge, while in the photograph below, troops are laying new rails.

One of the most sanguinary battles of the Civil War took place along the Antietam Creek on 22 August 1862. Major-General Ambrose E. Burnside advanced against the Confederate right wing over this bridge, but was thrown back by the sudden appearance of the Light Division commanded by Major-General Ambrose P. Hill.

while Jackson marched north to cut the railway communications behind their lines. Lee and Longstreet would follow a day later in order to effect complete surprise and to threaten Pope's depot at Manassas.

On 25 August, Jackson set off for the north, and the following evening occupied the Manassas magazines. On the 27th his troops plundered the railway trains loaded with supplies, destroyed everything else and withdrew. Pope could hardly let the chance slip to use his whole army to wipe out the enemy forces that were operating in his rear.

On 29 August, Union troops attacked the Confederates, who had entrenched themselves behind an unfinished railway line to the west of the old Bull Run battlefield. The Southerners found themselves under extreme pressure, but did not give way, as they knew that Longstreet was advancing from the west to reinforce them. Pope completely failed to recognize the fact that his left flank was acutely threatened – added to which certain mistakes were made by Brigadier-General Fitz John Porter – and when he reopened the attack on Jackson on the 30th, Longstreet ploughed into his flank, forcing him to retreat. The troops crossed the Bull Run in reasonably good order, with no signs of the panic of the earlier battle. At Chantilly, the advancing Confederates came up against the reinforcements from McClellan, and were brought to a halt. Lee was unable to make further progress towards Washington, although he had only lost 9,197 men as opposed to 16,054 men on the Union side.

Lee's successes during that summer were astonishing. Only three months earlier, in June 1862, had he taken over the command of the Army of Northern Virginia. In that comparatively short time, however, he had been able to move the war from his own capital almost to the gates of Washington. The Union retired to the fortifications around their capital after having lost the second Battle of Bull

Run, and had to abandon the whole of Virginia to the enemy.

Washington remained calm in spite of the defeat, and took the necessary steps for recovery. In a spirit of premature optimism, the Union had closed the recruiting offices in the spring of 1862, but hastily reopened them. The Virginia army was dissolved and the troops transferred to McClellan, while Pope was relieved of his command and sent to the West. Again it was believed that McClellan was still the right man, although many continued to doubt his capabilities. The ordinary soldiers on the other hand trusted him, as they were to trust no other general during the whole of the Civil War.

The Battle of Antietam. McClellan reorganized his Potomac army, and at the beginning of September 1862, marched with 97,000 men from Washington to

Soldiers of Company C of the 41st New York Infantry Regiment after the Battle of Manassas on 28 August 1862.

the north-west – six corps, a cavalry division and 300 guns. His plan was to find and stop Lee, who in the period 4–7 September had crossed the Potomac and advanced in the direction of Maryland. On the 7th, the latter stood with his army of some 55,000 men and 284 guns, at Frederick, Maryland, roughly 43 miles north-west of Washington. His nine divisions, divided into two corps under Longstreet and Jackson, were poorly equipped – the soldiers' uniforms were worn out and their weapons deficient. The Rebs could not count on supplies and had to live off the country. Their morale, however, was intact, and they regarded themselves as far superior to the Yankees.

The Union soldiers in turn were supplied with all their needs, they operated within accessible range of their ammunition supplies, and worshipped General McClellan. Why then did Robert E. Lee decide to invade the north of the Union under such unfavourable circumstances? One reason lay in the superb leadership of that great general and the high morale of his men. Another was that the Confederates were forced to attack the Union somehow and somewhere,

During the Battle of Antietam there was heavy fighting in a cornfield on the right flank of the Union army. These fallen Confederates were photographed after the battle by a Northern war correspondent.

in order to retain the initiative and to counter their enemy's power. It would only be a matter of time before the Union mobilized all its immeasurable reserves and overran the South. Lee hoped that by invading the fertile agricultural area in the North, he would gain much sympathy and dampen the North's ardour for waging war. It was also hoped that a victory would lead to international recognition of the South. If Lee's plan was successful, he would first cut the Baltimore and Ohio Railroad and then the Pennsylvania Railroad, thus isolating the Union from the east and the west. The most important cities, such as Baltimore, Philadelphia and also Washington, would then have to fall into the hands of the Confederates.

The initial stage of Lee's plan of campaign was to capture Harpers Ferry, which was defended by

12,000 men, in order to ensure the safety of his communications with Virginia. He divided his army, and on 9 September issued Special Orders No. 191. These provided for 'Stonewall' Jackson to withdraw back over the Potomac, and moving in a wide curve, to destroy the Baltimore and Ohio Railroad, finally ending up at Harper's Ferry. Further divisions would surround the latter from the north and the south. Matters did not quite work out as planned, however.

The orders landed up in the hands of the enemy, and McClellan was already reading them on the morning of 13 September. Everything thus depended on his readiness to march swiftly, and to inflict a surprise defeat on the widely spread Confederates. The South Mountains lay between his army and the enemy, and McClellan only needed to debouch from the two passes to divide Lee's forces and to defeat them individually. But McClellan, eternally cautious, only ordered his army to march on the following day, thus losing the chance of surprise and a decisive victory. In bitter fighting the Union army broke through the Confederate defensive positions, but the

'Bloody Lane' at Antietam. The Union troops threw their opponents out of this defensive position suffering heavy losses; Confederate corpses lie in the sunken road.

There was still a chance to defeat Lee, who at the decisive moment had only 20,000 men available. Again, however, McClellan believed that his enemy was superior, and he wasted too much time in arranging his line of battle.

On the morning of 17 September, the Union troops opened the attack, but in spite of great bravery, they could not penetrate the Confederate front. It seemed, that the Union would be victorious on the left, when at the last moment, the Southerners received reinforcements from Harpers Ferry. The Union army retired, and the bloody battle ended in a stalemate towards evening; 12,400 Union troops and 13,700 Confederates were killed or wounded.

The actual victory was won by the Confederates, who retained possession of the battlefield, and McClellan attempted no further attacks. From a strategic point of view, though, the Union had won, in that Lee's invasion of the North had failed. During

latter were able to rally on 15 September at Antietam Creek, near Sharpsburg. On the same day, Harper's Ferry had surrendered to Jackson, who then advanced to join the rest of the Confederates.

A doctor tends wounded Confederates after the Battle of Antietam.

the night of 18 September, the latter withdrew his damaged forces back to Virginia. The Union had retrieved the initiative, and in spite of further checks, the Yankees never abandoned the offensive until the war was ended.

The Confederate diplomatic campaign was equally wrecked by the indecisive result of the Battle of Antietam.

Five days later, on 22 November, President Lincoln laid the Declaration of Emancipation before the cabinet, and on the following day it was published. It stated that as from 1 January 1863, the slaves in the secessionist states would be regarded as free. This measure gave the Civil War the aspect of a crusade, as it was obvious to everyone that slavery would be totally abolished following a Union victory.

Although the British government was not convinced that the Union would ever bring the Confederacy to its knees, an intervention in favour of the South was not thought to be expedient. On 11 November, England refused to concur with a suggestion made by Napoleon III, whereby England, France and Russia should negotiate an armistice and the lifting of the blockade for six months.

Climax and end of the Confederate success in the West. The foregoing events were not influenced by the conflicts in the West, where the Union finally managed to assert itself, although the situation for the latter in the summer of 1862 appeared to be extremely threatening.

The responsibility for this state of affairs has to be laid at the door of General Halleck, who had taken over the command of the Tennessee and Ohio army on 11 April. General Grant was pushed to one side, and as Halleck's deputy had little to do, Halleck made the necessary preparations to capture the important railway junction at Corinth. He had some 100,000 men at his disposal, in contrast to the 35,000 of General Beauregard who was camped near Corinth. With such a superior force, Halleck should have been able to defeat and expel the Confederates throughout the West. His army, however, crept rather than advanced, giving Beauregard the opportunity to withdraw in time and evacuate the town on 30 May. The Union still had a chance though, by a swift advance on Vicksburg, to occupy the whole of the northern Mississippi. Such a march could only

have been stopped by Lee detaching a major troop contingent from the Army of Northern Virginia.

General Halleck, nevertheless, committed the unpardonable blunder of failing to press the offensive, which he further aggravated by separating his powerful forces into two divisions. General Don Carlos Buell was to move with the Ohio army to the east to capture Chattanooga in Tennessee, while General Grant remained to hold Memphis and West Tennessee. But General Buell wasted far too much time on the way to Chattanooga, rebuilding railway lines and defending them, with the result that he never got there. In addition, further troops were detached for other important operations.

In the meanwhile both sides suffered a change of command. On 11 July, Halleck moved to Washington as Commander-in-Chief, leaving Grant as Commander of the Tennessee Army. Grant and Buell, however, were independent of each other, so that the chaos became even worse. General Beauregard was ill, added to which he failed to get on with President Davis, so that he was relieved by Major-General Braxton Bragg.

The latter had more than 30,000 men in Chattanooga, while Major-General Edmund Kirby Smith was at Knoxville with 20,000. The Confederates then took the initiative. On 15 August, Smith left Knoxville, followed by Bragg from Chattanooga the next day. The plan was to advance north, reoccupy West Tennessee and capture Kentucky. Buell allowed himself to be outmanoeuvred by the enemy, and breaking off his railway reconstruction, he followed Bragg. On 2 September, Kirby Smith occupied Lexington, far to the north, and Grant had to detach four divisions to Buell in order to save the situation. On 16 September, Bragg took Monfordville, while for reasons unknown, Buell sat for a week in Nashville doing nothing.

In the West as in the East the situation looked black for the Union. In both areas, in spite of possessing the numerical superiority, they had permitted the initiative to be taken out of their hands. The Union generals had proved incapable of exploiting the advantages of an offensive. The North was more concerned with defending and retaining territory than in defeating the enemy.

Buell was to have been dismissed for incompetence,

but gained a reprieve as no better general could be found at the time. He then concentrated his forces, and on 3 October advanced with 60,000 men towards Perryville. Bragg, however, had splintered his forces, and sent his soldiers into Kentucky to recruit.

They had little success, as only a few signed on and the population showed little sympathy for the South. On 8 October occurred the Battle of Perryville in Kentucky. Although the Confederates only had 16,000 men, the Union was unable to decisively beat them. Both sides lost heavily – the Union 4,211 killed and wounded, and their opponents 3,396.

Bragg managed to re-assemble his army (60,000 men), and although he still had the advantage and his troops were veterans and confident of victory, he suddenly abandoned the campaign on 11 October and retired into Tennessee.

General Buell pursued the Confederates so

A Union railway gun at Petersburg.

hesitantly that he was replaced on 23 October by Major-General William S. Rosecrans.

In the meanwhile, General Grant had held his positions at Memphis and Corinth with 45,000 men. The Southerners reinforced their troops there, but were attacked by Grant on 19 September and forced to retire. In another engagement at Corinth on 3 October it again proved impossible to destroy the Southerners, but from then on, Memphis and Corinth remained firmly in Union hands. Grant had once again demonstrated that in the West there was a general who was prepared to attack the enemy under all circumstances, and this fact was noted in Washington.

After the Battle of Antietam, Lee was forced to retire from Maryland, and Bragg had abandoned Kentucky. In spite of many reverses, since the middle of October 1862 the situation for the Union had again become stabilized and all the Confederate advances had been halted. The awful threat of defeat had been banished, and the South was no longer in a position to be able to mount a co-ordinated offensive. The final advance of the Union was about to commence.

The Red Rover, *the first U.S. Navy hospital ship.*

Diplomacy during the Civil War. For both South and North, their relations with the two main European monarchies, England and France, were of great importance. Right from the beginning of the war it became apparent that the population of both countries tended to support either South or North according to their position in society. Workers, artisans and farm labourers believed in the triumph of the North as a victory for democracy, while the property owning and ruling classes were openly sympathetic towards the 'aristocracy' of the Confederacy.

The European aristocracy indeed would have been happy to see the break-up of the political system in America, as one more piece of evidence of the impracticability of democracy. The merchants in Europe were furious about the high protective tariffs imposed by the Union and which did not exist in the Confederacy. Shipping circles hoped for the total elimination or the destruction of the U.S. merchant marine, in order to be able to take over the merchant trade themselves. Although in Europe slavery was an anachronism in the second half of the nineteenth century, Great Britain did not have to have moral scruples on that point. The government in Washington repeatedly emphasized that the object of the war was to preserve the Union and not to solve the slavery problem. Thus when an envoy of the Confederacy pleaded for help from the European states, he could point this out. The politicians in Europe thus had a 'free hand' in making their decisions.

The Union was especially threatened during the first years of the war by intervention on the part of either Britain or France. Even prior to the bombardment of Fort Sumter, President Jefferson Davis had sent three envoys to Europe to plead for recognition of the Confederacy. Their mission, however, was unsuccessful.

Relations with the Union became critical during the so-called Trent Affair. The cruiser *San Jacinto*, under Captain Charles Wilkes, was on its way from Africa to the U.S.A., but put into St. Thomas in the Virgin Islands in October 1861 to take on coal, in the hope of encountering the cruiser *Sumter*, before finally returning to her home port. In Cienfuegos (Cuba), Wilkes discovered that two Confederate envoys, James M. Mason and John Slidell, were on the way to England and France, and would board the English steamer *Trent* in Havana for the voyage across the Atlantic. The latter set sail on 7 November, and Wilkes, knowing that she must pass through the Old Bahama Channel, lay there in wait. In the opinion of the cruiser's captain, a belligerent nation had the right to stop and search a neutral ship if he suspected that she was carrying enemy despatches. Wilkes gave a new interpretation to international law by defining the two envoys as being Confederate despatches. When the *Trent* was sighted on 8 November, he fired two shots across her bows and signalled her to heave to. A boat was sent across, and under the protests of her captain, Mason and Slidell were removed from the ship. Wilkes brought his prisoners into Hampton Roads, where he arrived with the *San Jacinto* on 15 November, and from there they were transferred to Fort Warren at Boston. In the North there was great jubilation at the capture of the two envoys. When the news of the affair finally reached England on 27 November, the Foreign Minister, Lord John Russell, proposed to send a stiff protest note to Washington, such as the Union would have been unable to accept. Queen Victoria, indeed, had no desire to provoke a war with America, so that the note was toned down before being sent with milder wording. On 21 December it was handed to the U.S. Foreign Minister, William Harry Seward. The latter, a lawyer, was an uncompromising opponent of slavery. He hated Britain, and before the outbreak of hostilities would have been glad to have provoked a war with Europe, in order to preserve the Union. Washington had to yield, however, and the reply sent by the U.S. Government was immediately accepted in London. Mason and Slidell were released on 1 January 1862, and permitted to depart for Europe.

Although relations had been strained during those weeks, other than sending troops to Canada, Britain had no intention of declaring war on the Union.

Strict neutrality was preserved during the course of the Civil War, in spite of official sympathy for the South. The latter were disappointed in their hopes, discovering that cotton was not the 'king', and certainly did not determine England's foreign policy. During this period there were a number of bad corn harvests in Europe, while those in the U.S.A. had been exceptionally good. As a result, Britain's imports of both corn and meat increased enormously. It was the latter products that were king, not cotton, and the Union was able to deliver both to Europe. Vital for good relations were the ambassadors in London and Washington. It was to the credit of the U.S. Ambassador in London, Charles Francis Adams, who had held the post since May 1861, that relations between the two countries remained normal. Through his understanding of the English mentality and his careful diplomatic behaviour, he succeeded in hindering the recognition of the Confederacy. Lord Lyons, the English Ambassador in Washington, also tried not to unnecessarily disturb good relations.

On account of the Confederate successes, it seemed in the summer of 1861 that their political situation would improve. Britain showed willingness to mediate, and in September 1862, the Prime Minister, Lord Palmerston, and Foreign Minister, Lord Russell, planned a cabinet meeting to agree such a step. Behind this was the view that if the Union rejected the offer, then the Confederacy should be recognized. In these considerations, however, one should not assume that hostility towards the Union was expressed. It was just that one wanted to be on the safe side in case of further military successes by Lee. The realities of the situation had to be accepted. Should the Confederacy finally win, it would have to be recognized as a new state on the American continent, and the war be ended through mediation.

Although this attitude showed great sympathy in principle for the South, London remained neutral for the time being.

After Antietam, Lee had to withdraw from Maryland, and Lord Palmerston and Lord Russell shelved their plans.

Right up to the end of the war, the Southern states had great difficulties in getting the ships out from Britain that they had ordered, and which were to be converted into warships at sea. Decisive for the non-recognition of the Confederacy was the result of the Battle of Antietam. The Southern advance was halted and their early successes in the West were wiped out. Even more important, however, was the Declaration of Emancipation that was announced by President Lincoln on 22 September 1862. This disposed of a convenient excuse that Britain might have used for intervention in the Civil War, and after 1 January 1863, all the slaves in the secessionist states were free.

Thus the war aims of the Union were more closely defined. They were fighting not only for the preservation of the Union, but for human freedom. Europe could no longer possibly think of supporting the South, and thus at the same time publicly condone slavery. On account of this brilliant gambit by President Lincoln, the South had lost the diplomatic war, and could only end it militarily.

Napoleon III of France also tried to arrange a six months armistice between the two warring parties in 1863, together with Russia and Britain. London and St. Petersburg, however, remained aloof. Finally, the French Ambassador in Washington suggested that

Emperor Napoleon III of France (1798–1873) tried without success in 1863 to mediate between the two warring sides.

both North and South should sit together at a table, to examine whether the war could be ended.

Congress replied angrily that any such suggestions would in future be regarded as hostile acts. At that time, Napoleon III was interested in Mexico, and persuaded Arch-Duke Maximilian of Austria, brother of the Emperor Franz Joseph I, to accept the Imperial crown of Mexico, supported by the presence of a French expeditionary corps. Under pressure from the Union, the French evacuated Mexico, so that Washington could mark up another diplomatic victory.

Astonishingly enough, Russia was friendly towards the Union. When, in 1863, tension occurred between Russia on one side, and Britain and France on the other, the Russian fleet moved to New York and San Francisco, and wintered there in 1863–4. If the European powers became involved in the war, the Russians planned to attack the commerce of England and France.

The Union was completely successful in ensuring that the Europeans did not become involved in the struggle on American soil. The North and the South were left to their own devices, and had to rely on their own resources to terminate the war in favour of one side or the other.

The diplomatic success of the Union lay to a certain extent in the fact that the U.S.A. was an already recognized state, and thus found it easier to establish her policies.

Still no decision. After the failure of the Confederate offensives in the summer and autumn of 1862, the main problem for the Union was to so concentrate her steadily increasing military and economic power, as to be able to crush the South. To achieve this aim, enormous difficulties had to be overcome. Three large armies were at the disposal of the Union:

(1) The Potomac army in Virginia.
(2) The Cumberland army in middle Tennessee.
(3) The Tennessee army in Mississippi.

Major-General McClellan was relieved of the command of the Potomac Army on 7 November 1862. After the Battle of Antietam he had remained more than a month north of the Potomac, and only re-entered Virginia on 26 October, after having been repeatedly urged to do so by President Lincoln.

His successor was Major-General Ambrose E. Burnside, who came from Indiana, where he was born in 1824. He passed out from West Point in 1847, but retired from the Army in 1853 to occupy himself as weapon manufacturer and railway employee. When the war broke out, he immediately made himself available to the Union, and as a brigadier-general in 1862, he was responsible for the capture of the strategically important Roanoke Island. With his appointment, the Union had again made an unfortunate choice. He even doubted his own capability to command a large army, and had not himself sought the promotion. He intended, however, to do his best, and knew that he was expected to produce victories – as soon as possible.

In planning his future operations, Burnside failed to realize that the Potomac army was in a favourable position for taking the offensive. It stood between the two halves of the Confederate army of Northern Virginia. Within a short while of the Battle of Antietam, Lee again had more than 80,000 men and 300 guns at his disposal. Confederate morale was still high, as up to then the Rebs had always been able to withstand Union attacks. Burnside made the

Major-General Ambrose Everett Burnside (1824–81) replaced McClellan as commander of the Potomac army on 9 November 1862. He was not a great general and lost the Battle of Fredericksburg on 13 December 1862, the worst defeat suffered by the Union. Seldom had a commander been so poorly prepared for a battle and fought it so badly. He was relieved of his command as early as 25 January 1863.

James Longstreet, both of whom were capable officers. The Confederate army had 75,000 experienced veterans, who were positioned some 3 miles from the right bank of the river among low hills prepared for defence.

Burnside started to cross the Rappahannock on 11 December, and attacked two days later. As was to be expected, his army was bloodily repulsed, losing 12,500 men. Even in the attack on Fredericksburg itself, the Union suffered heavy casualties. Famous features of that battle were the stone wall and the sunken road, so well defended by the Confederates that fourteen enemy attacks were repulsed – 6,000 Northerners were killed.

The Confederate losses totalled 5,300 men, and during the battle, their positions were not even seriously threatened. General Burnside wanted to repeat the attack the following day and to personally lead the columns, but his generals restrained him from such a suicidal move. Thus the Potomac army withdrew to the north of the river on 15 December, only to try to advance again five days later in mud and snow,

At the foot of Mary's Heights was a stone wall, behind which the Confederates were well protected. This enabled them to repulse a series of frontal attacks made by Union troops.

mistake of again advancing on Richmond, instead of defeating the separate corps of the Confederate army individually. It would have been far more important to defeat the enemy than to look for geographic gains and to capture territory. Burnside wanted to march from Warrington in Virginia, cross the Rappahannock eastwards at Fredericksburg and offer battle between the latter town and Richmond. The Union army – 120,000 men and 374 guns – reached the Rappahannock opposite Fredericksburg on 17 November. They did not cross the river immediately, but calmly waited for pontoon bridges to arrive, although there were several places where they could have reached the other bank without difficulty. The bridges did not arrive until 25 November. Burnside had allowed fourteen days to slip by without doing anything, while Lee used the time to make the necessary preparations to ward off the expected Union attack.

Lee was on the other side of the river together with Lieutenant-Generals Thomas Jonathan Jackson and

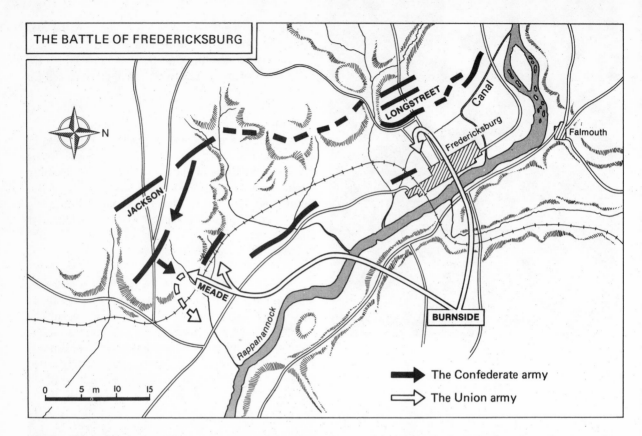

The Confederate army

The Union army

above Fredericksburg. The army became bogged down, and three days later gave up the effort. The mudbath was too much even for President Lincoln, who relieved Burnside of his command of the Potomac army.

He was replaced by Major-General Joseph 'Joe' Hooker. The latter, also known as 'fighting Joe', was born in Massachusetts in 1805. He also had studied at West Point, but left the Army in 1853 to become a farmer. At the beginning of the war he was a brigadier-general of the volunteers. In the earlier campaigns of the Potomac army, he had become conspicuous for his gallantry, but his supposed decisiveness deserted him as an army commander.

The war in Tennessee. In that theatre, things looked bad for the Union. The Ohio army under Major-General Rosecrans remained inactive for weeks, without attempting anything against Bragg's Confederates – who had again advanced north in the direction of Murfreesboro. Washington had to interfere to persuade Rosecrans to move, who finally broke camp on 26 December and marched south with a view to defeating Bragg. The latter had also

been subjected to hefty criticism from his own side on account of insufficient initiative. Thus it was that all of a sudden, both generals desired a battle. The Confederates stood with 38,000 men to the north-west of Murfreesboro, awaiting the Union advance.

On 31 December both sides attacked, and after a hefty struggle, the Northerners were pushed back to the Stones River. The Confederates, however, were not strong enough to achieve a decisive victory. The following day, both sides regrouped their armies that had become dislocated during the battle. Rosecrans stood with his back to the river in a dangerous position, but in spite of that his artillery managed to defeat a Confederate assault on 2 January. He had in the meanwhile been reinforced, and on the 3rd, Bragg withdrew south to Tullahoma. Major-General Rosecrans occupied Murfreesboro, but his army was so exhausted that it was a further six months before they were again in a position to take the offensive. Although the battle had ended in a draw, the Union had won a strategic victory in that Bragg had retired. The losses on both sides were heavy – the Union lost 12,906 killed and wounded, and the Confederates 11,740.

At the beginning of the war, most of the fighting fell to the lot of the volunteers. This photograph shows a Union volunteer in 1861.

The Tide of War Turns

Preceding pages. Sherman could not occupy the territory that he captured. In order to break the Confederate will to resist, all railway facilities and tracks were destroyed.

General U. S. Grant and the struggle for Vicksburg. The winter operations of 1862–3 had failed to produce a decisive success for the Union. Thus, further successful military operations depended on General Grant, who was a true fighter and would stop at nothing to achieve a planned target.

Grant occupied the western part of Tennessee, and had to defend Memphis as well as the railway lines that ran east and north-east from that city. The main aim was to capture the important town of Vicksburg on the Mississippi, so that his troops could unite with those in New Orleans and Baton Rouge. If he was successful, the entire course of the Mississippi

On 16 July 1862, the Confederate Ironclad Arkansas *slipped past the U.S. warships at Vicksburg and reached the fortress unhindered.*

from the source to the delta would be in Union hands, and thus the Confederacy would be split in two.

General Grant had 80,000 men, but roughly half of them had to be detached for garrison and occupation duties, so that only 40,000 effectives were available for offensive operations. His plan was to follow the north–south railway line that led to Jackson, the State capital of Mississippi. From there, he would march some 44 miles west to appear at Vicksburg.

The Confederate forces in the area were under the command of Lieutenant-General John C. Pemberton, who, on account of the fact that his wife came from Virginia, had gone over to their side at the beginning of the war. From November 1862 onwards, Grant pushed the Confederates steadily back, and laid down supply magazines along his line of advance.

During this time, Grant found out that intrigue was afoot in Washington. The 'political' Major-General John A. McClernand had promised President Lincoln and War Minister Stanton that if he was given command of an expedition against Vicksburg

Major-General William Tecumseh Sherman was one of the most capable generals of the latter part of the war. From 1862–3 he was Grant's right-hand man.

from the north, he would enrol the necessary troops. The Commander-in-Chief, Halleck, had appointed Grant to command the operation, and had given McClernand only a corps. The latter, however, was allowed to believe that he would take over the command.

Major-General William Tecumseh Sherman was given the mission, together with Rear-Admiral David A. Porter, of trying to effect a landing with transporters and gun-boats above Vicksburg and thus capturing the town.

Sherman, who came from Ohio where he was born in 1820, had taken part in the war with Mexico after leaving West Point. He left the army in 1853, but enjoyed little success in civilian life – six years later he became Superintendent of the Military School at Alexandria in Louisiana. In spite of his sympathy for the South, he offered his services to the Union at the beginning of the war. He took part in the first Battle of Bull Run, and as a brigadier-general was given command of the Department of Cumberland. During this time he criticized the incompetence of the government in Washington and got on the

wrong side of the powerful and influential Press. The latter accused him of being a madman – he actually was somewhat eccentric – with the result that he was relieved of his command. At the beginning of 1862, however, he was reinstated, and fought with Grant at Shiloh.

McClernand was given the order to advance with the gun-boats to Vicksburg, so that Sherman became his subordinate.

Grant believed that Pemberton would not be able to fight both himself and Sherman at the same time. If he moved against one of the Union armies, the other would attack his rear. In addition, the Union forces were superior in numbers to the Confederates.

Grant's plan, however, failed. Confederate

The Confederate cavalry leader Nathan Bedford Forrest (1821–77) was famous for his daring raids deep into Union territory, always defeating the enemy troops who were sent to stop him. Towards the end of the war, Forrest, who had entered the army as a private soldier, was promoted to Lieutenant-General.

Brigadier-General Nathan Bedford Forrest crossed the Tennessee and destroyed his communications and supply lines. The latter had joined the Southern army as a private soldier, and was feared for the rest of the war on account of his daring cavalry raids. On 18 December he cut the railway and telegraph lines to the north of Jackson with a cavalry regiment, so that Sherman advanced without McClernand on 20 December. Forrest looted so many weapons, horses and other items of equipment that he was able to completely outfit the recruits who were rushing to join him.

The Confederate Major-General Earl van Dorn was also able to operate in the northern part of Mississippi behind Grant's forces. On 20 December in a surprise action, he captured the supply depot at Holly Springs and destroyed stocks to the value of almost a million dollars. Sherman was also unsuccessful. The Union gun-boats and more than fifty troop transports arrived on 25 December at the mouth of the Yazoo River, to the north of Vicksburg. The following day the ships moved up the Yazoo in order to occupy the heights on the left bank and then finally the town.

In the meanwhile, Lieutenant-General Pemberton had occupied the strongly fortified heights of Chickasaw Bluff with 14,000 men. Sherman attacked there on 27 December, but three days later had to withdraw to Mississippi with heavy losses – 1,776 men killed, wounded and missing.

On 2 January 1863, McClernand took command of Sherman's troops, and moved up the Arkansas River with gun-boats to capture the Confederate Fort Hindmann, which surrendered on the 11th. He was ordered to return by Grant, and the whole Union army pitched their camp at Milliken's Bend, above Vicksburg.

General Grant had to realize that it would be almost impossible to capture Vicksburg from the north-east. In that situation, his lines of communication would be threatened. A better chance seemed to be offered by an advance along the Mississippi, especially as the Union gun-boats controlled the river to the north of the town. Thus Grant moved his headquarters to Memphis in order to be able personally to take command of the forces assembled near Vicksburg. On 30 January he moved to

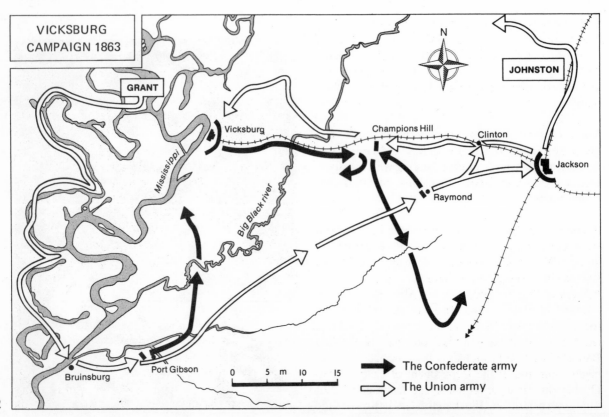

VICKSBURG
CAMPAIGN 1863

GRANT

JOHNSTON

N

Vicksburg

Champions Hill

Clinton

Jackson

Raymond

Mississippi

Big Black river

Bruinsburg

Port Gibson

0   5   m   10   15

➡ The Confederate army

⇨ The Union army

Young's Point, south of Milliken's Bend. It had become vital to concentrate the troops in the area and to make the best of a poor position. The Confederates were still in a favourable situation, determined to a certain extent by geographical factors.

Vicksburg lay on high ground on the east bank of the Mississippi, so that only an attack from the east or the south-east had a chance of success. On account of this, the Confederates had strongly fortified the left bank of the Yazoo which flowed into the main river to the north of the town. To the north of the Yazoo stretched an area of bayous (swampy streams) that cut up and sub-divided the whole countryside. An advance on Vicksburg through that obstacle seemed an impossibility.

Even to the south of the town, the terrain was hardly better. The Louisiana bank was flat, swampy and intersected with bayous. The Union army could only cross the river to the south with the help of gun-boats and steamers, which would first have to run the gauntlet of the Confederate forts. The latter had constructed batteries at all important points, to be able to hinder such a crossing. Grant had to solve the problem of how to capture the town from the east.

Following the earlier defensive successes, the Northern army came to a halt in the winter months of 1862–3. General Grant, however, did not allow himself to become depressed, and tried out several schemes to take the town. There were four possibilities, and Grant immediately commenced work on the first of these.

The powerful Confederate batteries that stretched five miles to the north and seven miles to the south did not permit the Union fleet to pass the town. At that point, the Mississippi made a sharp curve to the south-west, and a peninsula was formed opposite the fortress. Grant ordered Sherman's troops to dig a canal across the neck of this, in order to be able to pass out of range of the guns. The plan was abortive, however, in that the Mississippi refused to flow into the canal.

The second idea seemed far more promising. Roughly forty miles above Vicksburg was Lake Providence. Work was started on digging a canal from the lake into the Mississippi, so as to be

A Confederate battery at Fort Johnson in Charleston Harbor.

able to travel with ships down the Red River and re-enter the former below the town. This operation was soon abandoned, however, in addition to which there were no shallow-draught steamers available.

The third and fourth possibilities presented a chance to advance from the north with gun-boats into the Yazoo, to attack the flank of the fortified Chickasaw Bluff. If this were successful, the town would be bound to fall without further difficulty.

Firstly, the river bank at Helena on the Mississippi had to be broken through, in order to reach the Yazoo Pass via Moon Lake. On 24 February, the Union flotilla, which comprised the Ironclads *Chillicothe* and *Baron de Kalb* plus five small armoured gun-boats, all under the command of Lieutenant-Commander Watson Smith, entered the Pass. They were accompanied by a tug pulling three coal barges. A division of troops was embarked on thirteen transports, which were also protected by gun-boats. To have ensured success, they should probably have reached the Yazoo much more quickly, but Smith made slow progress. The Confederates used the time to erect 'Fort Pemberton' at Tallahatchie, which consisted of 73 earthworks protected by bales of cotton. To knock out that work, the two Ironclads with their 11-in. guns had to approach closely. The *Chillicothe* received several direct hits, and Lieutenant-Commander Smith declined to send in the *Baron de Kalb*. On 16 February, however, both Ironclads tried to silence the battery, and if successful, the troops would land and storm the fort. In the artillery duel, the *Chillicothe* was almost put out of action, and on the 19th the operation was abandoned. The ships retired the way that they had come, but on the way met reinforcements, and the new commander of the gun-boats, Lieutenant Foster, allowed himself to be persuaded to make another attempt to capture Fort Pemberton. Grant, however, ordered the troops to return, and they lay inactive in front of the defences. Rear-Admiral David A. Porter decided that in future he would lead such important operations in person. He surveyed a new route into the Yazoo, by way of Steele's Bayou.

On 14 March, the Ironclads *Louisville, Cincinnati, Mound City, Pittsburgh* and *Carondelet* entered the bayou accompanied by four tugs, each of which towed a bomb-vessel armed with a mortar. The ships had to struggle with all sorts of underwater obstacles

The U.S. monitor Carondelet *seen here on the Red River.*

in the muddy river bed, including trees that grew in the water. The enormous overhanging boughs of the trees along the river's edge, which were alive with snakes, damaged the superstructures of the warships. Troops guarded the Black Bayou against Confederate attacks, but the ships in Deer Creek made slow progress. Again and again the propellers were obstructed by trees in the water, the thin branches of which could only be removed with great difficulty. In the meanwhile, Admiral Porter found out from some Negro slaves that the Confederates were felling trees in the Deer Creek to block the further progress of the Ironclads. Soon the stream was completely blocked and the Confederates peppered the boats with rifle fire on 19 March. The guns of the Ironclads could not fire over the river banks, and General Sherman had to rush to their aid. By landing some guns, and with the help of the bomb-vessels, he was able to drive off the enemy, who retaliated by felling more trees in the rear of the flotilla to cut off Admiral Porter's retreat. This was further complicated when a coal barge sank in the narrow channel, with the result that his ships were trapped. Once again Sherman came to the rescue on 21 March. The barge was raised and the Confederate snipers chased off. Two days later the warships reached the Black Bayou and regained the Yazoo. The famous British military historian, Liddell Hart, called this operation the 'most romantically coloured adventure of the Vicksburg campaign'.

Although the operation was a failure, it was not entirely without its positive side, in that considerable quantities of cotton had either been destroyed or confiscated, and the Confederates had been forced to employ their reserves.

Grant did not lose heart at the series of failures to capture Vicksburg. In the meanwhile, however, the Northern newspapers were spreading the most improbable rumours about the campaign. Old stories were resurrected, and it was reported that an incompetent and frequently drunken general was in command. Grant knew that Washington badly needed a victory, and that a retreat would signify a terrible moral defeat for the Union.

Thus there was no other alternative but to cross the Mississippi to the south of Vicksburg, and at Hard Times, opposite the Confederate fortifications at Grand Gulf, there seemed to be a suitable place. To succeed, however, the army needed the support of Admiral Porter's warships. The operation to run the gauntlet of the Vicksburg defences with the Ironclads and transports began on 17 April, and in spite of heavy losses was a success. Both military and naval forces were thus positioned below the important strategic point.

On 30 April, Grant passed his army over the river at Bruinsburg, 11 miles to the south of Grand Gulf, while Sherman engaged the Confederates in the north. The latter fell back before the Union assaults and abandoned Grand Gulf on 3 May.

The situation for the South had become critical. General Pemberton took himself immediately to Vicksburg, and General Joseph E. Johnston, the supreme commander in the Western theatre, was ordered by Richmond to appear at the scene of events.

The problem for Grant was to hinder the Confederate troops around Vicksburg from uniting with those at Jackson, some 53 miles to the east. Vitally important also was the question of supply for the Union army. Grant decided to permit the soldiers to requisition – in other words, to live from the land – in order to make themselves independent, and for the coming march they were only issued with rations for three days. Grant's need was to lose no more time, and by rapid movement to defeat the two enemy armies individually. Because of this there was no time to build up a supply line, which could

anyway be cut by the Confederates. The march began on 7 May, with the advance of 41,000 men under Grant, to the north-east towards Jackson. The Confederates suffered their first defeat at Raymond on the 12th, while on the following day, Clinton, on the railway line between Jackson and Vicksburg, fell into the hands of the Union army. From there, Grant moved west towards Vicksburg. In contrast, Pemberton marched south to attack the Union lines of communication, which to his surprise did not exist. On the 14th, Johnston was forced to evacuate Jackson, and on the 16th, Pemberton's Confederate army was involved in the Battle of Champion's Hill.

The engagement was initially critical for the Union, but the situation was saved when Grant intervened. The following day the Confederates had to give way, and two days later the Union army was in front of Vicksburg. The siege began immediately, 30,000 Southerners being shut up in the fortress.

Thus one of the most brilliant operations of the Civil War was terminated. Even President Lincoln admired Grant's strategic capabilities, going as far as to say that even if Vicksburg was not captured, the campaign would rank as one of the greatest in world history.

The besieging force of some 34,000 men tried in vain to take the town by storm. The Ironclads bombarded Vicksburg, mines were exploded under the Confederate positions, trench mortars were used and hand grenades were thrown, but the garrison and the starving population refused to give in. Towards the end of June 1863, General Grant had more than 71,000 men at his disposal, and decided to mount a general assault on 6 July. This was forestalled by the unconditional surrender of Pemberton on the 4th. The garrison of 29,511 men were made prisoner.

With the fall of Vicksburg, the course of the Mississippi from the source to the Delta was under Northern control, thus dividing the Confederacy into two halves.

The Confederate offensive in the east – the Battle of Chancellorsville. Although the Union stranglehold on the South had been making itself more and more felt since the spring of 1863, it seemed as though there might still be a chance in the east of the U.S.A. for General Robert E. Lee to force his opponents to sue for peace.

At this time, General Rosecrans was still inactive in Tennessee, and Vicksburg was still holding out.

After the fiasco under Burnside, General Hooker reorganized the Potomac army. He especially ensured that the troops received enough supplies and that their camps were put in good order. More importantly, however, he restored their confidence in themselves. The cavalry was trained to such an extent that it could cross swords on equal terms with the enemy horsemen under the feared Major-General James Ewell Brown Stuart. Up until then the Northern cavalry had never been on a par with their opponents.

In the opinion of President Lincoln, General Hooker was far too optimistic about the result of the coming spring campaign. From the point of view of numbers, however, the Confederate position was becoming more and more unfavourable, while the Union received a steady stream of new regiments. General Hooker's army consisted of 122,000 infantry, 12,000 cavalry and 400 guns, while Lee had hardly half that quantity.

Hooker's plan seemed to promise success, and such a powerful army had never before been seen on American soil. He left roughly a third of his army at Fredericksburg, to tie Lee down. With the remainder, Hooker marched in a wide curve to the west, to cross the Rappahannock and the Rapidan 27 miles further west, to attack Lee in the rear. The latter would be thus forced to withdraw, especially as his lines of communication were threatened by Northern cavalry.

The move, however, failed to work out as planned. First, Hooker lost his nerve at the decisive moment, and Lee declined to behave in the way that the commander of the Potomac army had anticipated.

Soon the 70,000 troops who had left their positions at Fredericksburg on 28 April, were at Chancellorsville, an important road junction. The cavalry swarmed south in the direction of Richmond, but Lee did not permit himself to be distracted. Through his own cavalry under Stuart, who controlled all the approaches to Chancellorsville, he was well informed about the movements of the Union army. In contrast, General Hooker did not know where his opponent was, and thus remained stationary to the west of Chancellorsville.

Major-General Joseph Hooker (1814–79) was known as 'Fighting Joe'. On account of his supposed capabilities, Lincoln appointed him to command the Potomac army as the successor to General Burnside on 25 January 1863. During the Battle of Chancellorsville at the beginning of May, he suffered a defeat, and on the eve of Gettysburg he resigned his command.

General Lee demonstrated once again his sense of strategy, and his powers as a great commander. He divided his army into three parts in order to defeat the Union forces. One part remained near Fredericksburg to tie down the enemy forces there. Lee himself moved towards Chancellorsville with 45,000 men, while Stonewall Jackson advanced with 26,000 men to threaten Hooker's right flank from the south.

On 1 May, the Union troops attacked from the east in the direction of Fredericksburg, Hooker believing that he was taking Lee from the rear. The Potomac army, however, retired towards Chancellorsville, as the Confederate resistance was heavier than expected. Hooker had no idea of the enemy forces that opposed him – on account of the lack of cavalry reconnaissance – although he had, in fact, vastly superior numbers. He had 73,000 men on the spot and a further 17,000 possible reinforcements at Fredericksburg. As Lee was aware of the numbers opposed to him, he decided to attack the Union right flank, using Jackson's 26,000 men. The latter moved in a wide arc, so that by the afternoon he was behind the Northern army. Hooker had actually noticed troop movements, but assumed them to be a Confederate withdrawal. The Union was completely surprised and forced to retire, although the artillery was able to prevent a rout. During the night, Jackson, who wanted to take advantage of the success, rode out in advance of his forces, whereby he was shot in error by his own men. On 3 May, the Potomac army was in front of the Rappahannock and subject to strong Confederate attacks. Hooker could still have beaten them, as he still had 30,000 fresh troops who had not taken part in the battle, and at Fredericksburg the Confederate situation was critical.

General Hooker, however, lost his nerve. He resigned, and the command devolved on Major-General Darius Nash Couch. The engagements lasted until 6 May, when the Union army retired beaten over the Rappahannock. They had lost 16,792 men to their opponent's 12,754. Chancellorsville was one of the most impressive of General Robert E. Lee's victories.

The Battle of Gettysburg. After the Battle of Chancellorsville, the Confederacy, or rather General Lee, had regained the initiative, and the general was recalled to Richmond for consultations about further plans. Agreement was reached on an advance into Pennsylvania. They were quite correct to decide to remain on the offensive, but certain factors were overlooked that would ultimately lead to the failure of this daring operation. By advancing into the heart of the Union territories, the Confederates were risking everything on one bold manoeuvre. The Army of North Virginia, in spite of its high morale, was simply not strong enough to bring the campaign to a victorious conclusion. The Union would be forced to exert themselves to the utmost to defeat Lee, and already their superiority in manpower and materials guaranteed them the final victory.

If Lee were to be beaten, the superb Army of North Virginia would probably be destroyed, which would mean the end of the war for the Confederacy. They had, however, no other choice. If they failed to attack, the Potomac army would be reorganized and in its turn take the offensive. Additionally, the South still believed that as the result

of a victorious campaign, they would be granted international recognition.

The Confederacy still hoped that by threatening Pennsylvania, the Union would be forced to withdraw forces from the West, with the result that Grant would be unable to capture Vicksburg. It might have been better if Lee had remained in Virginia while reinforcements had been sent to the Western theatre. In that case, however, the South could rest assured that the Potomac army would invade Virginia. It was in no way disorganized, in spite of the many setbacks, and in spite of the poor leadership, the soldiers were in good condition. Thus Lee found himself on the horns of a dilemma. The Union had the strategic advantage, and would retain it until the end of the war. In view of the material superiority of the North, which increased daily, the Confederacy had simply no chance to force a decisive action and to end the war.

Lee's plan of campaign for the invasion of Pennsylvania was accepted in Richmond on 16 June 1863. With great secrecy, he had already started to march his troops north-west from Fredericksburg – a total of 76,000 men and 272 guns. The three infantry corps were commanded by the best of the Southern generals – Corps I by Lieutenant-General Longstreet, Corps II by Lieutenant-General Richard Stoddert Ewell and Corps III by Lieutenant-General Daniel Harvey Hill, while Stuart commanded the 12,000-man cavalry contingent. The Army moved up the Shenandoah Valley to cross the Potomac to the west of the Blue Ridge Mountains. Their advance was covered by Stuart's cavalry, while General Hill stayed behind at Fredericksburg to act as a decoy. It was not until 10 June that Hooker was informed that major enemy troop movements were in progress, and he initially had no chance to attack Lee's individual corps. He therefore informed Washington that he proposed to advance on Richmond, to force Lee to retire. Lincoln refused to agree and pointed out that his target was Lee's army, and not the Confederate capital. Ever since the Battle of Chancellorsville, Washington no longer had any confidence in the commander of the Potomac army. He was ordered to remain on the defensive, to follow Lee and to remain between him and Washington. On 13 June, General Hooker began to march north with 90,000 men, while on the following day, Lieutenant-General Ewell put 9,000 Union troops to flight near Winchester, and pursued 77 them into 15 June. Nearly half this force was taken prisoner.

On the same day Ewell crossed the Potomac at Shepardstown, and the following evening his advance patrols were at Chambersburg, the first Confederate troops to reach Pennsylvanian territory. Also on the 14th, Lieutenant-General Hill left Fredericksburg in the direction of the Shenandoah Valley, while Longstreet marched to the east of the Blue Ridge Mountains, to guard the passes.

Even further east, Stuart covered the Confederate advance. The whole time he was involved in skirmishes with Union cavalry, so that it was difficult for him to observe Hooker's movements.

Washington had reason to be worried by the threatening situation. President Lincoln called on the Union states to immediately enrol 100,000 militia troops, and ordered diversionary manoeuvres to try to force Lee to detach at least a part of his force. In Richmond, the government waited eagerly for news of further developments.

Hooker crossed the Potomac on 25 June, but did not possess the necessary breadth of vision. When he was still at Fredericksburg, he wanted to abandon the important Maryland Heights at Harpers Ferry, and with part of his army to threaten Lee's lines of communication and to attack him in the rear. General Halleck, however, insisted that Hooker should on no account divide his force. Like McClellan, the latter was convinced that he was not being given sufficient support, and that Lee possessed superior numbers. He therefore asked for permission to resign, and to his surprise, this was immediately granted – in spite of the threatening situation and the coming battle. On 28 June, he had to hand over command to Major-General George Gordon Meade. The Potomac army, which had thus far fought well under mediocre leaders, found itself with its fifth commander within ten months!

George G. Meade had been born in Spain in 1815, where his father had represented the interests of the U.S. Navy. After West Point, he had fought in Florida and Mexico, but at the outbreak of the Civil War had only reached the rank of captain. He soon became a brigadier-general of the volunteers, and took part in the fighting on the peninsula, at Manassas and Antietam. As a major-general, he

Major-General George Gordon Meade took over command of the Potomac army from Hooker on 28 June 1863, and immediately concentrated his efforts on forcing battle on General Lee. Under Grant, he retained command of the army, although the latter practically organized its operations during 1864 and 1865.

commanded a division at Fredericksburg and Chancellorsville. Meade complained about his new promotion, but saw it as his duty to halt Lee and bring him to battle.

His mission was hardly simple, as he had to cover Washington and Baltimore at the same time. Stuart had appeared with his cavalry before the capital on 28 June, and only a few miles away had plundered and destroyed 125 supply waggons.

Stuart was in no position, with three brigades, to attempt anything against Washington. His thrust, however, was a contributory factor to Lee losing the Battle of Gettysburg and thus the campaign. Stuart decided, with the help of the captured supplies, to swing far to the north around the Union army and then to reunite with Ewell in Pennsylvania. Because of the raid, Lee was without information about the movements of the Potomac army for ten whole days. Added to this was the fact that Lee's staff consisted of only a few experienced officers. He had no chief-of-staff and no other officer whom he could entrust with routine decisions. Stuart with his cavalry should have provided the commander with the necessary intelligence, but the former interpreted his imprecisely worded orders according to his own view of the situation.

Towards the end of June, the Confederate army stood on a line from Chambersburg to York with the three corps widely spaced out – a very dangerous position. Lee only found out that the Potomac army was at Frederick and on the way north on 28 June. Without his cavalry, his intelligence was more or less non-existent, and because of this he decided to concentrate at Gettysburg.

In contrast, Major-General Meade was well informed about the Confederate movements, and marched to Hanover, in order to occupy defensive positions between there and Westminster.

The two most celebrated Civil War armies were soon facing each other, each commander on the defensive and waiting for the other to open the attack.

On 30 June, the Confederates advanced to plunder a large store of shoes belonging to the Union, near Gettysburg, but stumbled up against the advanced posts of the enemy. They withdrew, with the intention of driving the Northerners out of the town on the following day. In the meanwhile, however, General Meade had realized the value of this important stores item, and as the Confederates moved in from the west during the afternoon of 1 July, they met determined resistance. The Battle of Gettysburg had begun.

On that day the main Confederate force stood to the west of the town, while more to the north were parts of Ewell's corps. The Union Major-General John Buford, who commanded the cavalry in front of Gettysburg, called for reinforcements, as he was being hard pressed by the enemy. In spite of bitter resistance, the Union troops were thrown back through the town.

To the south of Gettysburg, Major-General Oliver Otis Howard had assembled a reserve division on Cemetery Hill, where the retreating troops were able to rally and to defend themselves.

Towards evening on 1 July, Hill was to the west of

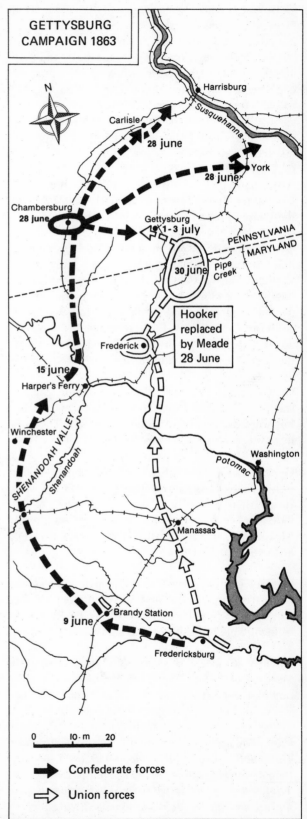

GETTYSBURG CAMPAIGN 1863

Harrisburg
Carlisle
28 june
Susquehanna
York
28 june
Chambersburg
28 june
Gettysburg
1 - 3 july
PENNSYLVANIA
MARYLAND
Pipe Creek
30 june

Hooker replaced by Meade 28 June

Frederick
15 june
Harper's Ferry
Winchester
Shenandoah
SHENANDOAH VALLEY
Potomac
Washington
Manassas
9 june
Brandy Station
Fredericksburg

0   10 · m   20

➤ Confederate forces
⇨ Union forces

Gettysburg, while Ewell occupied the town itself. General Lee was confident of victory on the following day, as up until then, things had gone well for the Confederates. Longstreet would head the main attack on Cemetery Ridge, while Ewell would occupy the Union right flank at Culp's Hill, and Hill would attack in the centre. Longstreet spoke out against an attack, as the Union forces had dug themselves into easily defended high ground, but Lee insisted on his plan being carried out.

After many delays on the part of the Confederates, Longstreet attacked frontally against the left flank of the Union, around four o'clock in the afternoon.

General Meade in the meanwhile had brought up more troops. When the storm broke loose at the southern end of Cemetery Ridge, the Northerners had to retire slowly back up the hill. In this critical situation, infantry and artillery reinforcements arrived in the nick of time, to pour fire into the advancing enemy. Both sides suffered heavy casualties, but the Union retained their positions.

On Cemetery Hill itself, the Confederate situation was no better. They succeeded in capturing the hill, but were driven off by a counter-attack. They did, however, succeed in occupying part of Culp's Hill.

General Hill's troops also attacked Cemetery Ridge, but at Gettysburg neither Ewell nor Hill displayed their usual initiative. The co-operation of the individual corps left much to be desired. As a result, Meade was able to transfer troops from the right and centre to his left wing.

General Lee overestimated the meagre successes of Longstreet and Ewell, and was confident of final victory on 3 July. Using fresh troops, he felt certain of being able to push in the Union flank.

After a struggle lasting several hours during the morning of 3 July, the Confederates were thrown out of the positions on Culp's Hill that they had

Casualties on the Little Round Top at Gettysburg. This small hill at the extreme end of the Union left wing almost fell into the hands of the Confederates on 2 July 1863. At the last moment reinforcements were thrown into the struggle and managed to retain this

important position.

captured the previous day. As a result, Lee decided to attack the Union defensive line to the south of Cemetery Hill, as he believed that the forces there were comparatively weak. If successful, the Potomac army would be split in two and their defeat would be unavoidable.

Again General Longstreet disagreed with the plan, but he had to yield. 15,000 men would advance from Seminary Ridge against the Union positions, supported by the fire from 170 guns.

The final day of the Battle of Gettysburg began at 13.07 hours on 3 July, with an artillery duel of such an intensity as had not previously been heard during the war. The batteries of the Union appeared to have been eliminated, and the Confederates were almost out of ammunition.

At around 14.00 hours, the Confederates, led by Major-General George Edward Pickett, advanced against the Union positions on Cemetery Ridge – climax and final defeat of the Confederate army at the Battle of Gettysburg. Between the two groups of hills was a unique spectacle, as thousands of bayonets glittered in the sun. The Union troops held their breath.

Once again, the Confederates were due for a disappointment. The Union artillery had not been silenced. During the preliminary bombardment, Brigadier-General Henry J. Hunt, artillery officer of the Potomac army, had ordered his gunners to hold their fire and only to open up again when the infantry began to advance.

The 200 Union guns wrought terrible carnage among the Confederate ranks, and the Northerners were amazed at the reckless courage of their opponents as they were simply shot down. The Confederate left flank collapsed and had to retreat, but the right flank managed to cross a stone wall and penetrate the Union line. Then, however, the reserves were thrown in and the assault was repulsed.

The Union won the battle by means of their superior power and better logistics. Brigadier-General Herman Haupt, the Director of Transport for the Union in the East, had managed to bring fifteen trains per day to the front from Baltimore, which were used to evacuate the wounded on the return

run. At that stage, if General Meade had attacked, the Confederate army would have been totally destroyed. But he, like his predecessors, lacked confidence, and was incapable of exploiting one of the finest opportunities of the whole Civil War, which he could have ended at one stroke.

After the terrible battle, General Lee once again demonstrated his excellent qualities as a leader, by bringing his survivors safely back to the South by 14 July – both officers and men retained their confidence in him.

The defeats at Vicksburg and Gettysburg, however, were the beginning of the end for the Confederacy. At Gettysburg, the Union lost *circa* 23,000 killed, wounded and missing, while the Southern casualties numbered some 28,000 men.

After the armies had retired from the battlefield, some 22,000 wounded from both sides remained behind. To care for them or to transport them to hospitals was an almost insurmountable problem. The doctors and ambulances had accompanied the Potomac army, and it was weeks before all the wounded had been attended to and carried away.

After the battle, it was realized that there was a further duty to perform, and the Union decided to lay out a cemetery for the vast number of dead. Pennsylvania proposed to found a memorial cemetery, supported by the other states, and which should be ceremonially consecrated. The impressive ceremony was held on 19 November 1863, and President Lincoln was invited to say a few words. His speech, however, was hardly noticed during the festivities, as he was not one of the main speakers. It was only later that it was recognized as one of the great documents of American democracy. He said:

'Four score and seven years ago our fathers brought forth on this continent a new nation conceived in liberty and dedicated to the proposition that all men are created equal.

'Now we are engaged in a great civil war, testing whether that nation, or any nation so conceived and so dedicated, can long endure. We are met on a great battlefield of that war. We have come to dedicate a portion of that field as a final resting place for those who here gave their lives that the nation might live. It is altogether fitting and proper that we should do this.

Four score and seven years ago our fathers brought forth, upon this continent, a new nation, conceived in Liberty, and dedicated to the proposition that all men are created equal.

Now we are engaged in a great civil war, testing whether that nation, or any nation so conceived, and so dedicated, can long endure. We are met here on a great battlefield of that war. We have come to dedicate a portion of it, as the final resting place for those who here gave their lives, that that nation might live. It is altogether fitting and proper that we should do this.

But in a larger sense we can not dedicate — we can not consecrate — we can not hallow this ground. The brave men, living and dead, who struggled here, have consecrated it far above our poor power to add or detract. The world will little note, nor long remember, what we say here, but can never forget what they did here. It is for us, the living, rather to be dedicated here to the unfinished work which they have, thus far, so nobly carried on. It is rather for us to be here dedicated to the great task remaining before us — that from these honored dead we take increased devotion to that cause for which they here gave the last full measure of devotion — that we here highly resolve that these dead shall not have died in vain; that this nation shall have a new birth of freedom, and that this government of the people, by the people, for the people, shall not perish from this earth.

The second version of the speech made by President Lincoln on the occasion of the consecration on the Gettysburg war cemetery on 19 November 1863. The writing is the President's own.

'But, in a larger sense, we cannot dedicate, we cannot consecrate, we cannot hallow this ground. The brave men, living and dead, who struggled here have consecrated it far above our poor power to add or detract. The world will little note nor long remember what we say here, but it can never forget what they did here. It is for us the living rather to be dedicated here to the unfinished work which they who fought here have thus far so nobly advanced. It is rather for us to be here dedicated to the great task remaining before us – that from these honoured dead we take increased devotion to that cause for which they gave the last full measure of devotion – that we here highly resolve that these dead shall not have died in vain, that this nation under God shall have a new birth of freedom, and that the government of the people, by the people, for the people, shall not perish from the earth.'

Confederate prisoners at Gettysburg. This battle marked a turning point in the war in that the Confederates were no longer in a position to be able to undertake any more large offensives.

Ironclads, Submarines and Auxiliary Cruisers

Preceding pages. A Union field telegraph at Wilcox Landing in the vicinity of City Point.

The bombardment of Charleston. As a result of the engagements between the *Monitor* and the *Virginia*, the Union decided on a building programme of monitors. With such warships they decided to master Charleston Harbor, which in addition to Savannah, was used by Confederate blockade runners. The operation, however, was not quite so simple as they imagined. The harbour, in the meanwhile, had been heavily fortified, and was difficult to capture from the direction of the sea.

The new monitors joined Rear-Admiral Samuel F. du Pont, the commander of the naval forces, in January 1863. Among them were the *Passaic*, *New Ironsides* and *Montauk*. The famous original *Monitor* had sunk in a storm on 21 December, on the way to her new operational area.

Together with three gun-boats and a bomb-schooner, Commander John L. Worden, captain of the *Montauk*, bombarded the Confederate batteries at Fort McAllister in Georgia on the Ogeechec River south of Savannah, on 27 January – nearby lay the auxiliary-cruiser *Nashville*. The idea was to test the effectiveness of the monitors' gunfire – which did not prove to be very satisfactory. During the bombardment, the *Montauk* received fourteen direct hits, without, however, suffering any serious damage.

Rear-Admiral du Pont remained sceptical about being able to soften-up Charleston with the monitors. Their rate of fire was far too slow, and it was difficult to aim with the turrets. How would it be possible to silence the 147 guns in the harbour entrance with nine monitors, when eight guns had been unable to eliminate Fort McAllister?

This scepticism, or perhaps pessimism, coupled with lack of initiative, was the reason for the U.S. warships' lack of success at Charleston. Navy Minister Welles was convinced that to get at the town, the ships would have to run the gauntlet of the forts and disregard any losses – Admiral Farragut would probably have carried out such a daring operation.

Preparations for the bombardment were complete at
the beginning of April. On the 7th, the monitors

As their warships were unable to silence the coast defences of Charleston, the Union resorted to a siege. They constructed heavy artillery positions on Morris Island, including the 'Swamp Angel' which could fire a shell weighing 200 lbs.

Weehawken, Passaic, Montauk, Patapsa, · New Ironsides (as flagship), *Catskill, Nantucket, Nahant* and *Keokuk* entered the harbour between Forts Sumter and Moultrie. Well aimed gunfire coupled with underwater obstructions and mines hindered a break-through, and several of the monitors were badly damaged. Towards evening, Admiral du Pont abandoned the attempt. The *Keokuk* had been hit ninety times, and sank the following day.

The bombardment of Charleston by U.S. monitors.

Du Pont intended to continue the attack on 8 April, but when he read the reports of the individual captains, he abandoned the idea. As a result, he was relieved of his command, and replaced on 4 June by Rear-Admiral Andrew Hull Foote. The latter died on the 26th, so that Rear-Admiral John A. Dahlgren assumed command of the Charleston monitors on 6 July.

The attack on the town was reopened on 10 July, by the *Catskill*, *Montauk*, *Nahant* and *Weehawken*, supported by troops under Brigadier-General Quincy A. Gilmore, who were landed on Morris Island. On the 18th, six monitors and five gun-boats managed to neutralize Fort Wagner, but the troops were unable to occupy it.

The bombardment lingered on into December. The monitors bombarded the town and the harbour almost daily, and fired some 8,000 11-in.- and 15-in.-calibre shells. The ships themselves received 882 direct hits, but the monitors proved to be efficient fighting units and were never put out of action. The operation demonstrated, however, that warships alone were unable to silence coast defences without the co-operation of an army on land.

Torpedo-boats and submarines. By this time a speedy victory for the South was no longer possible, although they had to try to resist for as long as they could. The Confederate Navy's mission was to break the ever tightening blockade, especially at Charleston, the most important Southern harbour.

Therefore, much energy was expended on the development and manufacture of mines, torpedoes, blockade runners, commerce raiders, Ironclads and even submarines. Owing to the lack of shipyards and machine plants, high-seas ships could not be built.

Both sides began constructing submarines at about the same time. In June 1862, the Union had a boat ready, which was christened *Alligator*, but after modification, it sank on 2 April 1863. As a result, the idea was abandoned, as the U.S. Navy swiftly rejected ideas that could not readily be effectively developed for combat.

Since the beginning of 1863, T. Stoney had been building a submarine at Charleston that could run

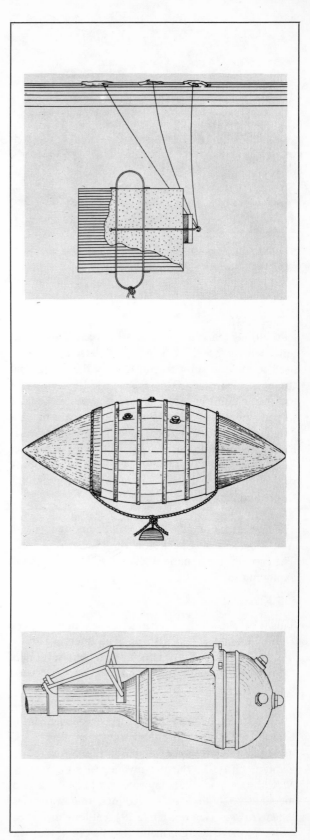

Three types of Confederate torpedoes (mines).

Confederate torpedo boats, known as 'Davids', were used mainly during the siege of Charleston.

The Confederate submarine Hunley. *Shortly after entering service, this prototype submarine sank during an engagement.*

half submerged. The boat was between 29½–49 feet long, with a beam of 5–6 feet. Ballast tanks were used to make it submerge until only the funnel and the hatch protruded from the water. In memory of the struggle in the Bible, this prototype of the later torpedo boat was called *David.* Her armament consisted of a so-called torpedo – a copper cylinder filled with an explosive charge of 11·34 lbs of powder – which was fixed on the end of a *circa* 14¾-feet-long projection at the front. The crew had to ram the target and explode the charge.

The first attack of a *David* was made on the Ironclad *New Ironsides* at Charleston on 15 October 1863. The captain, Lieutenant W. T. Glassell, succeeded in exploding his torpedo and lightly damaging his target.

This was followed by several unsuccessful attacks by *David*s against U.S. warships. The later history of the tiny torpedo boats is unknown, but several of them were found in the harbour when Charleston was finally occupied by the Union.

The Confederate Navy had a torpedo department at Charleston, where more than sixty men were working on new developments under the command of Captain Gray. In the meanwhile, Messrs. Hunley, McClintock and Watson were working on a submersible vessel at Mobile, Atlanta, that was christened *Hunley.* This was some 29½ feet long and 3 feet wide. To drive it, eight men turned a crank that was

coupled directly to the propeller. The ballast tanks were fitted at the conical ends, and illumination was provided by lanterns – the candles in them had the additional purpose of warning when the oxygen content in the boat dropped to a dangerous level. The trials of the first 'modern' submarine proved satisfactory, and the *Hunley* was transported to Charleston by railway on 7 August. There, the armament was modified, and at the bow, a protruding torpedo charged with 99 lbs of explosive was mounted.

During diving trials the boat sank several times, whereby thirteen men lost their lives, and General Beauregard ordered that attacks would only be made on the surface.

Lieutenant George E. Dixon was finally successful on the evening of 17 February 1864. The U.S. sloop *Housatonic* was anchored near Charleston, when a lookout discovered the approaching *Hunley*, which succeeded in placing and exploding her torpedo. The mortally damaged sloop immediately heeled over to port and sank within two minutes. Her attacker, however, also went down, taking with her the gallant crew.

Confederate auxiliary cruiser *Florida*. In England, Messrs. William C. Miller and Sons built a further auxiliary cruiser for the Confederacy, and on account of security the future warship was given the yard-name *Oreto*. The keel was laid in June 1861,

The Confederate auxiliary cruiser Florida *broke through the blockade in Mobile Bay on 4 September 1862, and in spite of suffering damage, managed to reach Fort Morgan.*

and in spite of the protests of the United States, she left Liverpool on 22 March 1862 under the command of a British captain, and arrived at Nassau in the Bahamas on 28 April. There, the Union tried everything to stop her departure, but she managed finally to leave on 8 August. The *Oreto* sailed to the uninhabited island Green Cay, where she took on her crew and armament from a waiting schooner.

She was commissioned as the Confederate cruiser *Florida* on 17 August by her captain, Lieutenant John Newland Maffitt.

The vessel displaced 700 tons, with a length of 197 feet and a beam of 26½. Her cruising speed was 9·5 knots and maximum speed under sail and steam was 12 knots. The armament consisted of two 7-in. rifled guns and six 6-in. guns.

On 12 February 1863, the Confederate auxiliary cruiser Florida, *commanded by Lieutenant Maffitt, captured the clipper* Jacob Bell *in West Indian waters.*

Lieutenant Maffitt first had to sail to Cuba, as he had yellow fever on board. Afterwards, he set a course for Mobile Bay to recruit crew members from the Southern states and to take on some missing guns. On the morning of 4 September, the cruiser lay off Fort Morgan in Mobile Bay, but as two U.S. sloops on blockade duty were also there, he had little chance to slip through.

Lieutenant Maffitt found himself in such a dangerous situation that he decided to try a trick, as his vessel was remarkably similar to an English warship. Initially, the sloops were not suspicious, and only became so when the *Florida* ignored warning shots.

Maffitt ran at full speed for Mobile, and it was too late for the U.S. warships to catch the Confederate cruiser. In the resulting engagement that lasted only 24 minutes, the *Florida* was severely damaged, but managed to reach shelter.

By 10 January 1863, she was again ready for sea.

The captain then had a crew of twenty officers and 116 men, as opposed to only twenty-seven when he had commissioned her.

To hinder the break-out, twelve blockading ships

The Confederate auxiliary cruiser Georgia *(600 tons) was commissioned on 8 April 1863 under the command of W. L. Maury. She took nine prizes in the Atlantic and on 28 October she was at Cherbourg. After coaling in England she was captured by the U.S. Navy on 15 August 1864.*

were assembled in Mobile Bay, but the *Florida* managed to slip out in fog and reach the open sea on 17 January.

On the way to Havana, she took her first prize on 19 January, and after coaling, Maffitt moved into the Caribbean on 22 January, where two further ships were captured.

On 27 January, the cruiser left Nassau where she had again taken on coal, and was followed for two days by the U.S. sloop *Sananoa*.

On 12 February, Maffitt succeeded in capturing the clipper *Jacob Bell*, whose cargo was worth some 1·5 million dollars. On 24 February she had again to coal, this time at Bridgetown in Barbados, where the crew were not allowed ashore as they had been deserting at every possible opportunity.

During the following days two more prizes were taken, and strong protests were heard in the U.S.A. about the evident incapacity of the Navy to deal with the Confederate cruiser.

Navy Minister Welles was doing all he could. He simply did not have enough ships at his disposal to carry out all his various tasks at once. Welles continued to regard his main duty as being to eliminate the Confederacy economically and militarily by means of the blockade, and did not permit himself to be distracted by the appearance of individual commerce raiders on the high seas. In those days it was extremely difficult without radio to discover the whereabouts of a cruiser operating alone, which could utilize all the hiding places throughout the world.

On 28 March, the *Florida* captured the bark *Lapwing* which Maffitt decided to use as a tender and armed auxiliary. It later became apparent, however, that she was unsuitable for such duty. Four more ships were destroyed during the following days, after which the cruiser put into Pernambuco, Brazil, where urgent repairs were carried out from 8–12 May. She met up with the *Lapwing* several times off the Brazilian coast, but the co-operation did not prove profitable.

In that area the *Florida* waged a successful war against Union commerce. Six ships were burnt and two others set free. Finally, the cruiser set sail for the North American coast where she reached the latitude of New York. There was a short fight with the U.S.S. *Ericsson* on 8 July, following which the commerce raider retired to southern waters. Several U.S. warships were hunting for the Confederate vessel, but they always arrived too late at the scene of action.

On 17 July, the *Florida* lay at Bermuda, and eight days later she left for France. On the way a further six ships were burnt and two permitted to go free. On 21 August, two days before she anchored at Brest, the *Florida* sank her last prize of the voyage. During her operations, the auxiliary cruiser had stopped twenty-three vessels, nineteen of which were sunk. Another fifteen were sunk by her various tenders.

The overhaul and repair of *Florida* took a considerable time, as spare parts had to be obtained from England, and the Union was doing everything within her power to hinder the work.

Lieutenant Maffitt was relieved, the command being assumed by Lieutenant Charles M. Morris on 9 January 1864. The *Florida* left Brest on 10 February and took on spare parts for her guns from a tug off Lorient. After that she went to Madeira and Teneriffe where, in spite of some difficulty, she was able to fill her bunkers with coal.

Morris then set a course for the West Indies, but the successes achieved were not on a par with those of the first voyage. It was not until 29 February that the first prize was taken, and although the cruiser remained in those waters until June 1864, her further booty consisted of only three sailing ships.

At the beginning of July, Morris moved to New England, where he managed to capture and burn six vessels. The *Florida* cruised off the American coast until the middle of the month, but the area was too dangerous on account of the many U.S. warships who were hunting for her.

Coal was then loaded in the Canary Islands for a voyage to Brazil, where the captain expected to find richer pickings. On 29 September, she took her last prize, before anchoring in Bahia to take on coal and supplies.

The blockade runner Robert E. Lee *was built in England in 1862. The ship undertook twenty-one voyages, bringing mainly munitions into the beleaguered South. After loading in Bermuda, she was captured on 9 November 1863.*

Already waiting in the harbour was the U.S. cruiser *Wachusett*, whose captain was Commander Napoleon Collins. Even at the risk of violating Brazil's neutrality, he did not let slip the opportunity to destroy his enemy. He attacked on 7 October, and after the *Florida* had surrendered, she was towed out of the harbour and brought back to the U.S.A. After a collision on 28 November in the harbour at Newport News, she sank in circumstances that have never been entirely clarified.

During her second voyage the *Florida* had stopped a total of thirteen ships, eleven of which were destroyed. She was the second most successful Southern auxiliary cruiser, and had caused the U.S. merchant navy to suffer losses totalling some 4 million dollars.

Confederate auxiliary cruiser *Alabama*. The most successful Confederate commerce raider was the

Raphael Semmes' commission as commander of the auxiliary cruiser Alabama.

Alabama. That ship, of 1,050 tons displacement with armaments of six 32-pdrs, two swivel guns, one 7-in. and one 8-in. gun, executed immeasurable damage – a total of 4,792,000 dollars. On 1 August 1861, the Confederate Naval Agent in Europe, James Dunwoody Bulloch, had signed the contract for the construction of the famous ship. Bearing the yard number 290, the *Alabama* was launched on 15 May 1862, although the Union tried every stratagem to hinder the delivery of the presumed Confederate cruiser. All their efforts were in vain, however, and on 28 July, 'Ship No. 290' left Liverpool with an English crew, en route for the Azores. There the guns and ancillary equipment were loaded, and on 24 August, she was commissioned into the Confederate service by Captain Raphael Semmes. The same day he left the Porto Praya Bay on the island of Terceira, in order to destroy the Union whaling fleet in the area.

The first catcher was seized and burnt on 5 November, and between then and the 18th, the *Alabama* destroyed eight more catchers and a schooner, to a total value of 230,000 dollars.

Raphael Semmes, captain of the Alabama, *became the Rear-Admiral in command of the flotilla on the James River towards the end of the war.*

The whaling season came to an end, and the remainder of the fleet departed, so that Semmes made tracks for the Newfoundland Banks, on the main shipping lane for the vessels carrying wheat to England.

In this new area of operations, the cruiser was able to capture eight prizes, while three sailing ships were permitted to continue their voyages. Semmes, however, felt that commerce raiding so close to the U.S. coast was too dangerous, and moved off in the direction of the West Indies. He decided to coal at Fort de France in Martinique, but because of the protests of the U.S. Consul, the authorities there made difficulties. The captain therefore sent his tender, which had followed him from England, to the coast of Venezuela. The following day, the U.S. cruiser *San Jacinto* arrived in the harbour at Fort de France, but in the evening, the *Alabama* was able to give her the slip in bad weather. Semmes then steered for the Gulf of Mexico, Haiti and Cuba – he was hoping to meet Union troop transports on their way to Texas, but was out of luck, and only one sailing ship was

sunk. His next project was to capture a steamer loaded with gold on her way from California to New York. On 7 December he stopped the expected steamer, only to discover that it was the mail liner *Ariel* with 500 passengers and 150 soldiers on board. Under the circumstances, Captain Semmes had to release her three days later.

After this, the cruiser was thoroughly overhauled at sea, and on 5 January 1863, Semmes headed for Galveston in Texas. He planned to hinder the landing there of Union troops and to attack their warships. On 11 January, the *Alabama* arrived, and from on board it was observed that Union ships were bombarding the harbour. Soon after, the paddle-steamer *Hatteras* (1,126 tons and five guns), which was serving on the blockade, approached the suspicious vessel. In the gathering darkness the *Hatteras* closed to within 20 yards of the auxiliary cruiser, before the latter opened fire. Thirteen minutes later the burning warship hoisted a white flag, and the captain and 117 crew members were rescued by the *Alabama*.

After that successful engagement, the cruiser moved to Jamaica to hunt for Union merchant vessels in the Caribbean. Between 26 January and 25 March, nine ships were captured and four released. In the meanwhile, the *Alabama*'s tender had returned to England on her own initiative and it was not until 4 April that Semmes could coal from the captured *Louisa* off the Brazilian coast. Near the island of Fernando de Noronha, in defiance of international law, two whale catchers were captured and burnt on 15 April, and another one ten days later. On 3 May, the cruiser encountered the *Sea Lark* which was carrying 550,000 dollars.

As the booty in the Atlantic was becoming scarce, Semmes then set sail for the Cape of Good Hope on 21 May.

On 20 June, Semmes put the bark *Conrad* into service as the auxiliary *Tuscaloosa*, to operate off the South African coast. Three further prizes were taken before the cruiser anchored at Cape Town on 5 August. That area of operation brought luck neither for the *Alabama* nor for the *Tuscaloosa*, with the result that on 24 September, Semmes moved off towards the Far East. On 6 November the first prize was taken near Java, followed by two more in the Sunda Straits. The ship was then overhauled at the island

Captain John Ancrum Wilson (third from left) with his officers on board the U.S. cruiser Kearsarge, *shortly after he had sunk the most successful Confederate auxiliary cruiser, the* Alabama, *in a gunnery duel off Cherbourg.*

of Pulo Condore, off Cochin China, and arrived at Singapore on 22 December. The previous successes had not been exactly overpowering, but the appearance of the Confederate vessel brought Union maritime trade to a standstill. His ship, however, needed

a thorough overhaul, so Semmes decided to return to the Cape of Good Hope, after which he would cruise off Brazil and then seek refuge in a neutral port to carry out repairs.

A few hours after leaving Singapore on 24 December, the *Alabama* captured a prize, and after an eventful voyage – three ships were destroyed on the way – she reached Cape Town on 20 March. Five days later the cruiser was again out in the Atlantic where two prizes were captured before she made fast in neutral Brest on 11 June. Semmes had to cope with all sorts of difficulties before he was given permission to overhaul his ship.

Already on 14 June, the U.S. sloop *Kearsage* arrived on the scene, commanded by Captain John A. Winslow, and with orders to destroy the *Alabama* at all costs.

Captain Semmes accepted the challenge, and left Brest on 19 June to attack the *Kearsage* (1,550 tons and seven guns), that was waiting out at sea. The Confederate cruiser opened the engagement at 10.57 hours, but was in every way inferior to her enemy.

Soon the *Alabama* was a helpless wreck, and after a gallant struggle, sank at 12.24 hours.

The Union uttered a sigh of relief. The most dangerous and most successful Confederate auxiliary cruiser had been eliminated, after having inflicted immeasurable damage. She had managed to destroy a total of fifty-five ships with a value of 4,792,000 dollars.

On 3 October 1862, the Confederate commerce raider Alabama *destroyed the sailing ship* Brilliant *with a cargo to the value of 93,000 dollars.*

Behind the Lines

(*Preceding pages*)
The heavy mortar 'Dictator' at Petersburg.

The Union and Confederate armies. In this terrible war it was the ordinary soldiers of both sides who had to bear the brunt of the fighting and share the horror of the slaughter. The Union troops especially, were poorly trained during the early months and led by incompetent generals, in spite of which they were regarded as excellent and tough fighters. From the point of view of the discipline of European armies, the troops of both sides were true individualists, who would not have submitted themselves to the barbaric drill of the Prussian system for example. Field Marshal von Moltke referred to the war as being fought by mobs, but even he could have learnt much from its lesson. After the preliminary problems had been overcome, the Americans developed into the most tenacious and finest of soldiers.

Right from the beginning of the Civil War, captive balloons were used for spotting troop movements. This picture shows the 'Intrepid' at Fair Oaks.

In the first months, thousands of Northerners and Southerners went to war filled with incomparable enthusiasm and optimism – which they soon lost. On account of the strong streak of individualism in Americans, it was quite natural that individual regiments for example, employed civilian cooks, to avoid having to eat army rations. In the South, a planter aristocrat would be accompanied by his personal servant. Volunteer regiments formed themselves as clubs; not everyone could join them. Orders were not necessarily obeyed immediately – they would be first discussed and sometimes those involved came to blows with their officers. In time, however, the soldier had to give up much of his accustomed freedom of will in order to fight and thus to survive. The ordinary private realized that his life might be positively or negatively influenced by the decisions of his superiors. He thus learnt to obey, but never wanted or accepted the blind automatic obedience of his European counterpart. He was given a lot of leeway by the officers – who also enjoyed their independence and like their subordinates, were also Americans.

Besides individualism, another reason for the supposed loose discipline lay in the fact that the officers

The headquarters of the 50th New York Pioneer Regiment at Petersburg.

were either elected by the soldiers or appointed by the State Governors – mostly for political reasons. As a result, the officer was keen to be popular and accepted by his subordinates. Apart from this, in the early part of the war, the officers understood little about military life, so that officers and men had to rely to a great extent on each other. They all learnt the art of warfare empirically, and in so many bloody battles proved that courage, discipline and soldierly conduct were needed to advance into the face of murderous enemy fire. The Civil War soldier should be numbered among the best in history. The officers who were incapable of learning to lead their men, and who failed in other ways, soon departed from the scene. The solid core of officers and men whose loyalties survived the realities of combat formed incomparable armies.

March and battle formations were difficult skills to acquire. For example, to form a division on the march – in four files 1,500 yards in breadth – lines had to be formed, each of which might be spanned by the frontage of one or two regiments. Ten companies of a regiment marched forwards in ten parallel columns – each column consisting of two files some 40–50 men in depth. The columns were then obliged to wheel left or right into the firing line, advance or turn about and retire perhaps across broken ground and under fire.

Marksmanship was not developed on the range, as it was believed that every ordinary American was an expert rifleman. This notion was for the most part a myth. True though, some of the Southerners expecially had experience of fighting the Indians and gun handling in their farming communities; but many of the troops had never fired a weapon before their first battle, and understood little about effective ranges; a factor that was to prove fatal for many of them. Right up to the beginning of the war, the basic tactics for Regular infantry armed with smooth-bore muskets with a range of little more than 50 yards, had been to advance right up to the enemy and to scatter them with a bayonet charge.

The personal weapon of the Civil War soldier, as in Napoleon's time, was still a muzzle-loader, but the 99 barrel was rifled to give it a range of some 800 yards. An advancing enemy line could thus be met at a considerable distance by murderous fire. One result was that during the war, defenders tended to dig themselves trenches or to seek shelter behind hedges – in other words, every possible use of cover was exploited. A frontal assault on a fortified line if not doomed to failure incurred heavy casualties; fifty years after the war was over the same lesson was to repeat itself with further tragic consequences in the war in Europe 1914–18.

Both North and South suffered heavy losses for the reason that in spite of improved fire power, Napoleonic tactics were still employed.

The bulk of the artillery were also muzzle-loaders with a calibre of $4\frac{1}{2}$ in. and above, firing a ball weighing $3\frac{1}{2}$ lbs. The range of such weapons was about one mile, which was enough for defence against infantry attacks, especially in the hilly and wooded countryside of North America. In addition, there were

already some 3-in. rifled guns that could be effectively used for counter-battery fire against the muzzle-loaders, over a greater range.

Both types were directly aimed, in that the crews had to see the target with their eyes. Indirect fire was at that period unknown.

Large mortars were employed against fortifications, as plunging fire was impossible with the normal guns. There was also heavy siege artillery, which from the technical point of view, was not particularly well designed.

Because of their industrial capacity, the Union possessed more and better artillery than their opponents, who, in contrast, had excellent cavalry during the early part of the war. During hostilities, the Union had a total of 7,892 guns at their disposal.

The bulk of the Southern soldiers came from country areas, and were experienced with horses and took their own animals to war. It was therefore no wonder that they had the best cavalry generals – Brigadier-General John Hunt Morgan, Major-General Joseph (Fighting Joe) Wheeler and the

Union heavy siege artillery. This piece was known as 'Whistling Dick'.

famous Major-General Nathan Bedford Forrest who had had no formal military training and had joined the Confederate army as a private soldier.

In spite of many engagements and brilliant raids, the cavalry played a subsidiary role in the Civil War – mainly used for reconnaissance and for covering troop movements.

Besides infantry, cavalry and artillery, there were the engineers, a particularly important branch. They constructed bridges, roads, fortifications, pontoon bridges, railway lines etc. Demolitions and mine-laying also formed part of their duties, although these were often carried out by the front line troops themselves. In that respect, the Union had a definite advantage. Among the Northern troops were many artisans and craftsmen, and there was hardly anything that they could not carry out under the guidance of an expert engineer officer.

Exactly how many soldiers served in both armies is no longer possible to state with any accuracy, as the statistical material available is highly contradictory. In the Union army roughly 2·1 million men served altogether, of which there were some 75,000 regulars, 1·9 million volunteers, 460,000 were conscripted and 73,000 joined up as substitutes.

The strength of the Confederates is even more difficult to quote. The figures given vary between 600,000 and 1·5 million men. Taking the three year period of service as a basis, we come up with a total of 1,556,678 for the Union and 1,082,119 for the Confederacy.

For the individual years we can quote the following figures:

	Union	Confederacy
July 1861	186,751	112,040
January 1862	575,917	351,418
March 1862	637,126	401,395
January 1863	918,121	446,662
January 1864	860,737	481,180
January 1865	959,460	445,202

The economy in war. Like all the later modern wars, the American Civil War was not decided only by one side having better soldiers than the other. Indeed, the economic and industrial potential of the adversaries had a decisive role to play. The military strengths of both the Union and the Confederacy solely depended on the economic structure of their individual territories. Right from the outset, the North had an advantage over the South, of which it was not initially aware. Vast industrial resources were at the disposal of the Union, which meant that in spite of early defeats, she would ultimately win the conflict. The South was incapable of fighting a modern economic war, as there, the industrial revolution had been resisted, and the rural economy was based on the support of slavery. Industrialization was to prove decisive in winning the war.

To replace the men who had joined the army, the South drafted slaves for work in the fields, but this measure was not enough to promote victory. Slavery had hindered the training of artisans and craftsmen, and compared with the North, the networks of communications had only been primitively developed.

During the war there was no longer any possibility of extending road and railway systems, so that the distribution of supplies broke down. In addition, industrial poverty made it necessary to close down certain railway lines.

The North. Both factions suffered greatly from inflation. Neither had been prepared to wage war either militarily or financially. In 1864 for example, the Union had to raise three million dollars per day to pay for the cost of warfare, and living costs rose enormously. Profiteers exploited the situation, and their greed drove prices higher and higher. By 1865, the load had become almost unbearable, especially for the ordinary people in the North.

A result of the economic boom was that prices rose more quickly than wages. From 1861–6 for instance, wages increased by 10 per cent. while prices went up by 50 per cent. The profiteers and swindlers did well out of this, for example, by selling shoddy goods to the government at staggering prices.

The politics in Washington contributed to the fact that the financially powerful firms controlled capital after the war. Many famous organizations, such as Armour (meat packing), Huntingdon (railways), Remington (rifles), Rockefeller (oil), Carnegie (iron and steel) etc., laid the foundations of their future wealth in the Civil War. A vast boom broke out in the North. Initially it had been thought that on account of the war, trade and industry would be reduced, but the opposite proved to be the case – an experience that was equally felt by the belligerent powers in the twentieth century.

During the first year, times were hard, as the economy had still not recovered from the 1857 crisis. The North lost 300 million dollars that was owed to them by the South. The Federal government, however, rapidly mobilized the economic reserves and spent enormous sums on the army. Already in the summer of 1862, the economic recovery was being felt everywhere, and in Philadelphia alone in the years 1862–5, 180 new factories were built.

The Northern farmers, who, prior to 1861 had largely sold their products to the South, were also favourably placed by the war and no longer needed to hunt for markets for their produce.

The government, however, bought not only corn for the army, but vast quantities of leather for shoes, textiles etc. There was absolutely nothing that the State did not require, and production rocketed.

Although in the North, many farmers and their sons had volunteered and joined up, there was no shortage of agricultural labour. The industrial revolution was responsible for bringing new machines on to the market such as the steam thresher and mowing machine, thus simplifying farm work. Added to this was a steady increase in the land devoted to crops.

In 1862, Washington passed the Homestead Act, whereby every settler could obtain 160 acres of land for a minimal sum, which after five years would become his property. On account of this, some 15,000 new farms were created during the war.

Equally important was the stream of immigrants from Europe. In the years 1861–2, immigration sank below the 1860 level; but then began a new stream of arrivals and more than 800,000 people flooded into the U.S.A. Hardly any of them went to the South, as even before the war, immigration into that area had been minimal.

The agriculture in the North was not only able to supply the needs of its own people, but those of Europe as well – especially England which was the destination of 40 per cent. of the wheat exports.

Corn had overtaken cotton in importance. England was thus unable to declare war on the Union, as it would have meant a shortage of food.

During the early war months, manufactured goods were still being bought overseas by the North, but already by 1862, hardly any orders for munitions were being placed in Europe. The iron industry – mainly in Pittsburgh – was geared to produce enormous quantities of guns, mortars, railway tracks and steel for warships and locomotives.

The well planned network of railways, that was greatly extended during the war, played an important role in the Civil War, as the Union armies could easily be transported from place to place. The railways fulfilled an important strategic need; Brigadier-General Herman Haupt commanded the U.S. trans-

The iron works at Fort Pitt in Pennsylvania were indispensable for the Northern war effort. The Civil War caused a boom in trade and industry.

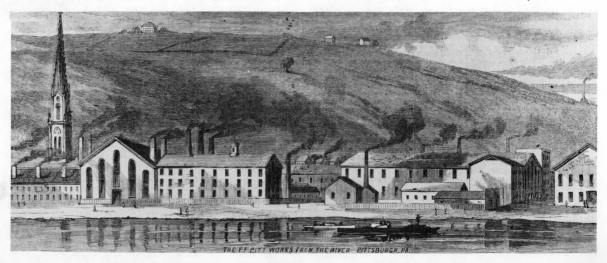

THE F.F PITT WORKS FROM THE RIVER PITTSBURGH.PA.

port and railway construction department with great ingenuity.

During the war, a protective tariff that had been so bitterly argued about, especially in the South before 1861 was adopted. The Northern scheme was not only to raise tax revenue, but also to protect the local economy from European competition.

The Union financed its expenses, however, during the war mainly by war loans, issuing *circa* 450 million dollars of paper money (so-called green-backs), which were not supported by gold reserves. Their value hovered around 39 cents in actual metal. Prior to 1861 there had been no income tax in the U.S.A., but personal taxes brought in comparatively little. Also no tax on consumer goods had previously existed. The first step was to double the customs duties and then a direct tax was imposed on so called luxury articles, such as alcohol and tobacco. Coupled with the new income tax, these measures brought in a total revenue of 675 million dollars – in other words, less than the cost of one year of war.

Loans were necessarily raised abroad, and so Washington was in this way able to pay three-quarters of the war bills.

The South. In contrast the Southern economy completely collapsed. The inhabitants, however, gave their government more and demanded less than their Northern counterparts. Richmond was scarcely in a position even to supply their troops with the bare necessities.

The South at first, made the mistake of trying to involve England and France in their cause by withholding the cotton harvest. Had they not done so, they could have used the profit to lay in a stock of weapons and other vital goods. The Union blockade later negated all their efforts to remedy the situation by shipping the crop abroad.

The Confederacy was therefore forced to feed itself, which was feasible but for the fact that the Richmond government lacked organization. In spite of this, it was remarkable just what was achieved, although all efforts were in vain as far as the outcome of the war was concerned.

Cotton planting had to give way to corn and vege-

Brigadier-General Herman Haupt was responsible for the construction of military railways and for transport generally. He resigned from the U.S. Army in 1863 but remained as advisor on railway matters.

tables; and salt pans, textile factories, gunpowder plants, shipyards etc., had to be laid down. The Tredegar Iron Works in Richmond was the main arsenal in the South. Raw materials were so short, nevertheless, that scrap metal had to be procured to manufacture ammunition. As a result of these efforts, the Confederacy succeeded in waging war for four years, an amazing feat.

Worse, was the early collapse of the communication systems. In 1861, the Confederacy had 960 miles of railroad track, as opposed to rather more than 27,000 miles in the North; moreover, only 4 per cent. of the locomotives were built in the South. There were few Southern railway repair facilities. Through lines were rare, so that goods often had to be off-loaded and transported by horse cart from one terminus to another. Although railways played an important role in the war, it was not until February 1865 that the Confederate Congress made funds available for new construction. During the course of the war, the few rolling mills were so busy with orders for weapons, that there was no free capacity 103

for locomotives, waggons or track. Therefore, the less important lines were closed down, the rolling stock was transferred to other areas, and the track was torn up for use elsewhere. Towards the end of the war, the railway material in the South was so antiquated that the average speed of a train was only 7 miles per hour.

The shortage of supplies for the troops and the civilian population can largely be blamed on the collapse of the transport system.

In addition, the industrial facilities of the South became more and more vulnerable to the slow but inexorable advance of the Union armies.

The Union troops destroyed according to plan all railway lines, factories, workshops and farms, so that they would no longer be available to the Confederacy. Towards the end of the war, the Rebs had weapons and ammunition, but little else. They were obliged to loot shoes, uniforms and food from fallen or captured Yankees.

Southern profiteers and racketeers existed who sold

The blockade runner Rattlesnake (*formerly the auxiliary cruiser* Nashville) *sought refuge under the guns of Fort McAllister in the Ogeechee. She was destroyed there on 28 February 1863 by the monitor* Montauk *and three gun-boats.*

the luxury goods brought in by the blockade runners at a great profit.

Right from the outset, the financial position of the Confederacy was unfavourable, and in 1861 only a million dollars was available in cash. The taxed income was negligible, and the inhabitants had little intention of paying up. The enormous gap between income and expenditure could only be bridged by the issue of bonds and banknotes, which would be paid back when the Confederacy was recognized as an independent state. As there was no backing in gold for this issue, its value steadily declined. At the beginning of 1864, a Confederate dollar was only worth 4 cents, and by the end of the year it was valueless.

The inflation took on monstrous proportions. In Richmond in 1863, for example, a pound of butter cost 4 dollars. The daily wage of a factory worker, however, was 3 dollars, while a soldier was paid 11 dollars per month (the Union soldier received 13 dollars). As a result of the increase in prices, the population became steadily impoverished.

In spite of total economic collapse in the Confederacy in early 1865, the troops fought to the bitter end with astonishing loyalty and endurance.

Only desperate resolve held the Confederacy together, until it was defeated by the stronger forces.

The Negro question. Every modern war has brought in its train a change in society. These conflicts have motivated hopes that could no longer be restrained. Compromise has no longer been acceptable, and this applied especially to the American Civil War. Each side demanded victory as a vindication of its ideals and aims, and the longer the war lasted, the less the

During the action at Fredericksburg (December 1864) the town was almost entirely devastated by the Union artillery.

respective governments were inclined to abandon their concepts – either a reconstituted Union without the right of secession, or an independent Confederacy with a semi-feudal society. Therefore both sides were prepared to accept any method and means that would ensure victory.

The Union, out of necessity the agressor, had no other aim than to defeat the South. A negotiated peace could not be considered; the enemy had to be totally defeated.

As soon as the Union concerned itself, though, with the Negro or slave question, the very foundations of Confederate society were to be shaken to the core.

Although President Lincoln had issued the Declaration of Emanicipation on 22 November 1862, whereby all the slaves in the Rebel states would be free as from 1 January 1863, he still had not won approval for this step from the Army and the civilian population. The soldiers were fighting for the preservation of the Union, not for the abolition of slavery. Slowly, however, as the military situation

altered in favour of the North, the Union troops themselves realized that the South must be subjugated in order to ensure her defeat. The Yankees regarded slaves as Rebel property that assisted the Confederate war effort. As a result, if taken from their owners and treated as contraband, it was both logical and practical to set them free. Thus the abolition of slavery resulted less from the Declaration of Emancipation, than from the advance of the Union army liberating the slaves in order to destroy the Confederate states. Coupled with freeing the slaves from their masters was the destruction of private property, especially in the West where the Union advanced steadily. Barns full of corn were burnt, unoccupied houses went up in flames, cotton was destroyed, bridges demolished and factories were flattened. In this respect General Sherman's Tennessee army was particlarly active, as many ruthless soldiers served under his command.

The liberated slaves voluntarily followed the Union troops, but nobody knew what to do with them.

Initially they were housed in camps that were guarded by the Negroes themselves, but then someone came up with the idea of utilizing their labour, and Negro regiments were formed. By the end of the war 300,000 coloured troops were enlisted, although only some of them took part in actual combat – 2,751 fell in action.

In the South, Negroes were employed as army labourers, but not as soldiers, although towards the end of 1864 both President Davis and General Lee were in favour of a limited use of coloured combat troops.

A law was passed in May 1865 which provided for the call-up of 300,000 slaves, but as the war was nearing its end, only a few companies were formed. Nobody discussed freeing the slaves in return for their contribution to war service.

The emancipation of the Negroes resulted in awkward problems, that have still not been solved in the U.S.A. today. From an economic point of view a speedy liberation was impractical. Millions of former slaves, mostly illiterate, without trades or any form of property, were free and moved to the North, where they were not wanted. The landless and impoverished Negroes simply wandered about, whereas in the South they had at least had work.

The black man was left with no other choice than to sell his labour cheaply, thereby provoking the hatred of the whites, especially middle and lower classes; racial antipathy was the unfortunate result of the Declaration of Emancipation. President Lincoln would have liked to have seen his coloured population transported to Africa, but the Negroes wanted to become full U.S. citizens and were reluctant to return to their unfamiliar 'homelands'.

U.S. cavalry orderly at Antietam.

106

Grant Leads the Union near to Victory

Before Sherman left Atlanta to march to the Atlantic coast, everything of military value was destroyed. The photograph on the preceding pages shows railway lines being pulled up.

The battles at Chickamauga and Chattanooga. After the capitulation of Vicksburg, the Union army paused awhile. Grant was of the opinion that he could move as far south as Mobile, through the southern part of Mississippi and Alabama, without meeting serious resistance. Washington, however, was obsessed with the idea of occupying as much Confederate territory as possible, with the result that Grant had to detach part of his army.

President Lincoln showed himself to be especially interested in an occupation of East Tennessee, as the population there sympathized with the Union. General William Starke Rosecrans remained with his Cumberland army in Murfreesboro (Tennessee) after the Battle of Stones River, to reorganize his army. The Confederate General Braxton Bragg was camped with the Tennessee army some 40 miles away at Tullahoma.

After being repeatedly urged by Washington, Rosecrans finally resumed his march on 23 June 1863, with the aim of capturing Chattanooga and of supporting the operations of General Burnside, whose mission was to bring Knoxville and East-Tennessee under Union control. Bragg, whose army had a strength of some 47,000 men, had to withdraw, and abandoned Tullahoma, where Rosecrans lingered a further eight weeks before resuming his advance on Chattanooga on 16 August.

Chattanooga was the gateway to the south-east of the Confederacy. From there, the only direct railway line to Virginia ran to the north-east via Knoxville; the Memphis and Charleston Railroad also ran via Atlanta to Georgia and Carolina.

A demolished railway bridge on the line between Nashville and Chattanooga. A Union pontoon bridge crosses the river near Bridgeport in Alabama.

Rosecrans accelerated his operations towards Chattanooga, and thereby manouevred extremely cleverly. He went round the Confederate defensive positions to the north and north-west of the town, by following the railway line from Tullahoma in a southerly direction. When his army reached the Tennessee river and the railway at Stevenson and Bridgeport (Alabama), he swung east and threatened Bragg's lines of communication. The latter had to abandon Chattanooga on 7 September, and two days later his opponents occupied the town.

Then, however, Rosecrans made the fatal mistake of continuing to advance, rather than establishing his defences and refreshing his troops. His three corps became separated in the mountain passes, while Bragg remained stationary about 20 miles to the south and absorbed reinforcements.

The corpse of a Confederate soldier in a trench at Petersburg.

President Davis became extremely worried about the threatening military position in the area, and sent by railway two divisions from the Army of Northern Virginia under General Longstreet – with the result that Bragg had 70,000 men as opposed to Rosecrans with only 58,000 men.

The latter collected his dispersed troops as swiftly as possible, when the veteran Confederate army stationed along the Chickamauga Creek went on to the attack on 19 September. After bitter fighting, the Union army was defeated, and its retreat turned partly into a rout. The next day, however, Major-General George Harry Thomas managed to halt the Confederates at Snodgrass Hill, earning by his brilliant defence the nick-name of 'Rock of Chickamauga'.

Both sides suffered heavy casualties – the Cumberland army lost 1,657 killed, 9,756 wounded and 4,757 missing, while Bragg's figures were 2,312 dead, 14,574 wounded and 1,486 missing.

As a result of the lost battle, the Union army found itself besieged in Chattanooga. Rosecrans was relieved of his command, being replaced by Major-General Thomas.

Bragg was criticized for not having exploited his victory to the utmost, but President Davis, who came to Tennessee, confirmed him in his command.

As a result of the unhappy outcome of the Battle of Chickamauga, it was realized in Washington that there was no longer any point in occupying Confederate territory at any price. Grant was ordered to assemble all available troops to relieve the garrison of Chattanooga, that had already been put on half rations. The Confederates had invested the town in a large semi-circle – from the north on the Tennessee along Missionary Ridge to the south, and then west to Lookout Mountain where the Southern line regained the river.

In the north there was a mountain road from Chattanooga to the west that was held by Union troops, but which could not be used for bringing in supplies. The only possible way of supplying and relieving the besieged army under Thomas, seemed to be either over the river, along the railway on its southern bank, or via the roads in the south. All these ways, however, were controlled by the 111

Confederates, who only had to wait until the garrison was forced by hunger to surrender.

The Union could simply not allow a defeat at Chattanooga, and threw in reinforcements, whereby the railway system played a decisive role. General Hooker loaded two corps from the Potomac army in goods waggons, which took six days to travel the distance of almost 1,300 miles; General Sherman was also on the march eastwards from Memphis.

On 3 October, General Grant was ordered from Vicksburg, where he lay ill. War Minister Stanton personally handed him the orders that made him commander of all the Union forces between the Mississippi and the Alleghanies, and made him responsible for resolving the crisis at Chattanooga.

The new commander arrived in the town on 23 October. Within four days a road had been opened to Bridgeport in the north-east, while Hooker arriving from the west had united with the forces under General Thomas. A few hours later the first supply waggons were rolling into Chattanooga over a pontoon bridge across the Tennessee River. On 23 November, Sherman arrived with 20,000 men from

Potomac army soldiers in the vicinity of Fredericksburg.

his Tennessee army, which gave Grant a total of 61,000 against Bragg's 40,000. The latter had sent General Longstreet off to the north to drive the Union troops out of Knoxville with 20,000 men on 4 November. As a result he had decisively weakened the Confederate forces and sent one of the best generals off on a useless errand.

On 24 November the Union army moved to attack the strongly fortified Confederate positions. General Hooker forced the enemy off Lookout Mountain whereupon they retired to Missionary Ridge. General Sherman did not progress very far in the north (on the Confederate right wing), so that on 25 November, Grant ordered Thomas to drive the Southerners from the slope of Missionary Ridge.

The same afternoon the Cumberland army not only stormed the slopes, but with great bravado, the fortified ridge itself. Within a short space of time, Bragg's right wing was destroyed and the Confederates retreated in panic. The Cumberland army broke out in jubilation over their victory, and in the resulting confusion, it was no longer possible to organize a pursuit of the defeated enemy.

In the Battle of Chattanooga, the Union lost 735 killed and the Confederates 361.

Sherman immediately marched to Knoxville, which he reached on 6 December, only to find that Longstreet had departed two days earlier.

The beaten Confederate army retired to Georgia.

The South had thus lost the war in the West, and in the spring of 1864, Union pressure would increase sharply – the Southern States no longer had a chance to delay the final defeat in this theatre.

General Grant appointed Commander-in-Chief. On 9 March 1864, Major-General U. S. Grant was received by President Lincoln and was promoted to the newly created rank of lieutenant-general, in addition to being appointed Commander-in-Chief of all the Union forces. In Grant, the President had finally discovered the general who was capable of bringing the war to an end.

Lincoln had realized, after so many unfortunate attempts, that an expert was required for solving the military problems. Grant would mobilize the

Major-General U. S. Grant in the autumn of 1863.

Major-General Nathaniel Prentiss Banks marched from Louisiana in March 1864 to advance in the Red River area in Texas, in co-operation with Rear-Admiral David Dixon Porter. The Army was supported by thirteen monitors and seven smaller gun-boats. The aim of the expedition was to requisition the cotton stored in the area, and to dissuade the Emperor Napoleon III from his Mexican adventure which was regarded as a threat by the Union. The campaign was poorly prepared and had to fail – it ended in fiasco. The troops under Banks were beaten at Sabine Cross Roads on 8 April, and again on the following day at Pleasant Hill. Banks retreated so precipitately that his expedition nearly ended in a catastrophe. At that time of the year, the Red River suffered from low water, and enormous efforts were required to get the monitors and gun-boats back to their starting point – a dam even had to be built.

On 20 February, the Northerners under Brigadier-General Truman Seymor suffered defeat in the Battle of Olutee in Florida, when white and black troops in a badly planned operation attempted to win back the area for the Union.

Brigadier-General William Sooy Smith was also

resources of the Union, and in an unceasing struggle would exhaust Robert E. Lee's Confederate army and force it to surrender. In future under Grant, there would be no more long pauses after battles and time wasted until the next offensive. He accordingly proposed to exhaust the enemy reserves by means of continuous fighting. The following battles demonstrated, however, that in spite of superiority in *matériel* and manpower, the Union was unable to destroy the enemy in a decisive engagement. The fire power of well concealed troops – on both sides – negated any frontal attack, and the only way to force the Southerners to retreat was to turn their flank.

Although Grant achieved the final victory, his military talents should not be overestimated. He was not a great general, but was tough and resolute, and in spite of the terrible losses suffered under his command, he retained the confidence of the Union army.

Subsidiary campaigns. In the other theatres of war, the Union suffered some defeats on account of dispersal of effort, which could otherwise have been avoided.

The disastrous Red River expedition began on 12 March 1864. It was commanded by Major-General Nathaniel Prentiss Banks who was supported by mortars and gun-boats, one of which was the 523-ton monitor Osage *armed with two 11-in. guns.*

After a series of engagements in which many soldiers lost their lives, the Red River expedition ended with the retreat of the Union forces. At that particular season the level of the river was extremely low, with the result that the army under Lieutenant-Colonel Joseph Bailey had to build dams in the neighbourhood of Alexandria so that the warships could be brought out. The picture shows material for the dams being brought up by the U.S.S. Signal.

defeated by the Confederates on 22 February, commanded by the famous General Nathan Bedford Forrest, in an engagement in Mississippi. Under Grant, such operations that were not in any way decisive and were strategically pointless, were stopped. He was not interested in occupying towns and supposed strategic points. His aim was to beat the enemy by any means possible and without dissipating his resources.

Two Southern armies had to be eliminated, then their destruction would spell the end of the Confederacy. One was the Tennessee army of 60,000 men, commanded by General Joseph E. Johnston (Bragg had in the meanwhile been relieved), which lay at Dalton in Georgia, not far from Chickamauga. The other and more important army was commanded by General Robert E. Lee, who had concentrated his 60,000 men below the rapids in central Virginia.

Grant's strategy. The Union progressively set about dividing their enemy, so that each group would be unable to exist independently.

The command in the West was given to Major-General William Tecumseh Sherman.

The Tennessee army under Major-General James B. McPherson was based at Chattanooga. Under the same overall command was General Thomas's Cumberland army as well as the smaller Ohio army of Major-General John M. Schofield – a grand total of 100,000 men.

As Commander-in-Chief, Grant attached himself to the Potomac army, which was still commanded by Major-General George Gordon Meade, although the former became responsible for its operations.

Major-General Henry Wager Halleck remained behind in Washington, relegated to desk duties as Chief-of-Staff.

A new member of the Potomac army was Major-General Philip Henry Sheridan who had served with skill in the West at Chickamauga and Missionary Ridge. He became the cavalry commander.

The Union army was camped near Culpeper Court House on the north bank of the Rapidan. Attached to it were the troops under Major-General Ambrose Everett Burnside, so that Grant had more than 120,000 men at his disposal.

In the south, near Fort Monroe, were the 33,000 men of the James army commanded by Brigadier-General Benjamin Franklin Butler. His mission was to march north along the southern bank of the James in the direction of Richmond, while Grant would advance to the south. The latter believed that the advance of the James army would force the Confederates to send reinforcements to Lee.

Major-General Franz Sigel (who had emigrated from Germany to the U.S.A. in 1848) was to march with a division from the Shenandoah Valley to the east over the Blue Mountains to Richmond.

Grant's plan foresaw that in spring 1864, three Union armies would move in a concentrated attack on the Confederate capital, while Sherman with another three armies would advance on Atlanta in Georgia. The Confederates would be unable to oppose this crushing superiority – they were no longer in a position to be able to assemble new armies or to replace the coming losses.

The Battle in the Wilderness. The advance began on 3 May – 105,000 men of the Potomac army moved south to cross the Rapidan. Grant's plan was to offer battle to Lee south of the so-called Wilderness. Grant, however, underestimated Lee and the Southern will to resist as well as the geography of the area.

The Wilderness was some 13 miles long by 7 miles wide, and spread directly out from the southern bank of the Rapidan. In earlier times the trees in the area had largely been felled for use in charcoal smelting ovens. As a result the undergrowth had become so thick that in the course of time it was almost impenetrable and one could hardly see ahead for more than a few yards; few paths and clearings were in evidence.

General Lee undertook no measure to hinder the Union troops from crossing the river. His soldiers were much more at home in the Wilderness than the Northerners, and he purposely chose this inhospit-

On 4 May 1865, the Potomac army under Grant set off to march south and crossed the Rapidan at Germana Ford.

able and impenetrable area as a battlefield. It was his opinion that his army, inferior in numbers but still imbued with fighting spirit, should be able to halt Grant's forces there and to beat them.

Thus, on the evening of 5 May, the two day Battle of the Wilderness began, characterized by incredible and terrible scenes. During the bitter fighting, the undergrowth caught fire, with the result that the wounded were either roasted alive or mutilated when the paper cartridges in their belts exploded. Neither side could see for more than a few paces, and nobody really knew whether they were advancing or retreating. Smoke and fire darkened the sky, and the situation for the Union became extremely critical on more than one occasion – it really seemed that Lee would destroy the Potomac army, but the Northerners managed to hold the daring and desperate attacks of the Confederates.

On the evening of 6 May, the struggle was at an end. Both sides tried to extinguish the fires in order to rescue the wounded. The Union casualties were 2,246 killed, 12,037 wounded and 3,383 missing,

while those of their opponents totalled about 12,000. Tactically, Grant had been defeated in that he had not reached his objective, and he realized that he must not give up, but rather try to regain the initiative. Much to the amazement of the soldiers, therefore, the Army marched the following day further south instead of retiring to the north, as had been the previous practice of the Potomac army

The Battle in the Wilderness was characterized by the large number killed. The Union wounded were brought to Fredericksburg.

after an indecisive engagement. Grant decided to try to force Lee to retire by making a flanking movement, and his objective was Spotsylvania Court House, from which position a road led to Richmond.

The Confederates, however, arrived at the spot only a few moments after the Northerners, and thus blocked Grant's further advance. Out of this situation developed the Battle of Spotsylvania that lasted from 8–20 May. The ensuing engagements demonstrated over and over again how impossible it was to advance by frontal assault against the well

Casualties being evacuated during the Battle in the Wilderness.

entrenched Confederates. Real trench warfare developed, and both sides were unable to drive their opponents from the trench systems even with enfilading fire. The conflict was especially fierce at Bloody Angle, where the Union nearly succeeded in breaking through on 12 May. The Potomac army was not always lucky under General Grant. The chain of command was chaotic – just as it had been in the Wilderness – local successes were not exploited and orders were carried out far too slowly. It cannot be denied that the Confederates were far better able to exploit a favourable tactical situation, or to react to developing danger, than their opponents. Losses on both sides were again enormous, but Grant was in a better situation to cope with them than Lee. Grant tactically could afford a battle of attrition, but rather than sacrifice more men piecemeal, he wanted to force Lee into an open conflict. In the twelve day battle, the Union lost 14,267 men, while the Confederates lost 6,000 killed and about the same number were captured.

On 20 May, the Union army again moved further south, forcing Lee to withdraw to avoid being taken in the flank. On 27 May, the Northerners crossed the Pamunkey, while the Confederates worked on their defensive positions at Cold Harbor, only a few miles away from Richmond. In these engagements, Lee repeatedly demonstrated his strategical and tactical capabilities, hindering Grant from imposing his army between the Confederate forces and their capital. The Southern army occupied, with 55,000 men, an excellently constructed line of trenches roughly seven miles in length, and were opposed by

as many as 100,000 Yankees. Grant thought that he could break through the line in one massive frontal assault, but on 3 June, the attack crumbled within five minutes in the face of the Confederate fire. Within an hour the Union had lost between 6–7,000 men, while 1,500 of their opponents were killed.

General Grant abandoned the useless assault, and the armies lay facing each other in the trenches for a further nine days.

Until then the Union army had covered nearly 70 miles from the Rapidan to Cold Harbor and the suburbs of Richmond. In spite of this, Grant had been unable to destroy Lee's army in open battle. Lee, however, was incapable of repulsing his opponent or of forcing him to withdraw, which up until then had always been the case with the Potomac army. Each general had found in the other a worthy opponent, although Grant retained the initiative. The Union had lost 54,929 men in the battles from Wilderness to Cold Harbor, in other words 52 per cent. of the fighting strength of the Potomac army (105,000 men). Against this, Lee had lost 39,000 from 61,000 men, which represented 59 per cent. of his forces, and could not reckon on further reinforcements. 'Stalemate' was equivalent to battlefield massacre.

The failures of the other Union armies. In the meanwhile the other Union armies had achieved nothing. The Army in the Shenandoah Valley under Sigel and the James army commanded by Ben Butler, had commenced operations according to plan on 4 May, but within two weeks everything had gone wrong. The plan was for Butler to advance with 36,000 men from City Point on the James to Petersburg. Instead   117

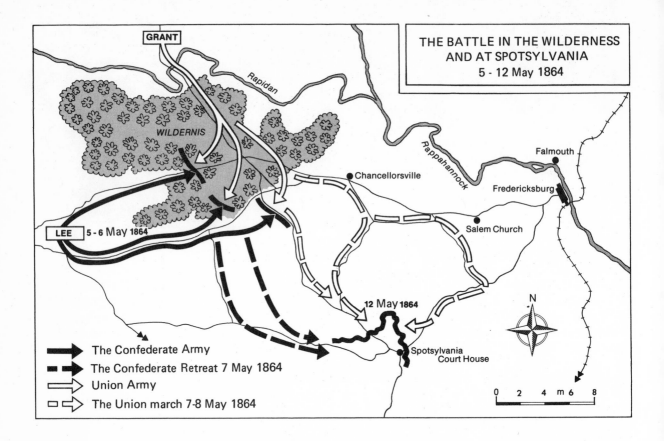

THE BATTLE IN THE WILDERNESS
AND AT SPOTSYLVANIA
5 - 12 May 1864

The Confederate Army

The Confederate Retreat 7 May 1864

Union Army

The Union march 7-8 May 1864

of doing so, he concentrated his forces at Bermuda Point where he was shut in by the Confederates.

Sigel's task in the Shenandoah Valley was to occupy the enemy forces in south-west Virginia, so that they would be unable to detach reinforcements and send them to Lee. Sigel, however, was defeated on 5 May at New Market.

Grant advances on Richmond. After the Battle of Cold Harbor, Grant intended to cut off Lee's forces from Richmond. Firstly, however, the important railway junction of Petersburg, to the south of the Confederate capital had to be captured.

In a brilliant manoeuvre, the Potomac army was disengaged from the trenches at Cold Harbor during the night of 12–13 June and marched to the south to cross the James River. The planning was excellent, and by 1 June that whole army was on the southern bank.

It should then have been possible to capture Petersburg and force the Confederates to surrender. But through irresponsible delay, Major-General William F. Smith lost a unique chance to capture the lightly held town (some 2,400 men), as early as 15 June. The fortifications had looked impressive, but were only thinly occupied. An initial attack by Smith had some success, but he decided to wait for the following morning before mounting the main assault.

In the meanwhile, General Beauregard succeeded in bringing up reinforcements, and Lee moved up with his troops. The following Union attacks which were to a certain extent carried through without much energy and enthusiasm, all failed. It was the same story as in the preceding weeks. It was impossible to penetrate defensive positions manned by the Confederate veterans, in a frontal assault. Part of the failure must be apportioned to Grant, who had ordered the less energetic General Smith to capture the town – he should have known that Smith was unsuitable for such an important task. Grant had to settle down to conduct a siege of the town, little realizing that it would drag on until 2 April 1865.

In the north there was disappointment over the lack of success of the Army under Grant. War-weariness was spreading, and the lengthy casualty lists were greeted with great concern.

For the last time, Confederate troops under Major-General Jubal Anderson Earl advanced along the Shendandoah Valley from June to August 1864, almost reaching Washington on 11 July. Grant, however, sent reinforcements, and under the eye of a worried President Lincoln, the attack by Earl's 13,000 men was defeated. He withdrew, but always managed to throw off the pursuing Northerners.

The campaign in Georgia. On 5 May, W. T. Sherman started his march from Chattanooga to Atlanta. The bulk of his army consisted of combat experienced veterans and he was also able to rely on his generals. – George H. Thomas with the 61,000 men of the Cumberland army; James B. McPherson with the Tennessee army (24,500 men) and John M. Schofield with the smaller Ohio army (13,500 men).

A view of the primitive fortifications at Petersburg.

Sherman was opposed by General Joseph E. Johnston who had 60,000 experienced troops, but with no chance of repelling the enemy advance. His only hope was that the Northerners would assault his defensive positions and thus suffer bloody noses for their pains.

Sherman, however, utilized the terrain for manoeuvre and conducted a series of flanking movements. Johnston was a clever tactician who always retired when he recognized danger. When the Confederates dug in, McPherson and Schofield tried to surround their positions, but Sherman was unsuccessful in bringing Johnston to battle in favourable circumstances.

The Battle of New Hope Church from 25–28 May was indecisive, and it was not until 27 June that Johnston offered battle at Kenesaw Mountain. Sherman attacked, but was repulsed with the loss of 3,000 men.

The flanking movements were continued, with the result that after two months, the Northerners arrived in front of Atlanta on 9 July. On the 17th, Johnston

On 15 June 1864, the Union failed to capture the sparsely defended and poorly fortified Petersburg, with the result that the war was lengthened by nearly a year. A form of trench warfare ensued, similar to that in the First World War, and this photograph shows a Confederate works.

was relieved of his command by President Davis for not having stopped Sherman. He was replaced by General John B. Hood as commander of the Tennessee army, but in the struggle for the town from 20 July to 1 August, he could do nothing to save the situation. Sherman's army succeeded in cutting the railway line that supplied Atlanta by means of a wide flanking turn. After a furious struggle in which McPherson was killed, Hood evacuated Atlanta during the night of 31 August, and the following day the town, already largely destroyed, was occupied by the Union army.

Behind the fronts. In the summer of 1864, both Jefferson Davis and Abraham Lincoln had many worries. Lincoln was not convinced that he would be re-elected, and thus felt that the Union might end the war and the Confederacy become independent.

President Davis, who possessed an iron will and great determination but who was also arrogant, did not doubt the justice of the Confederate cause.

The Confederate General Jubal Anderson Early penetrated into the suburbs of Washington with his troops in June 1864.

During the march to Atlanta under Sherman, the Union army came up against the well constructed Confederate position at New Hope Church, some 27 miles to the north-east of the city. Here also a form of trench warfare resulted.

On 2 June 1864, the Cumberland and Tennessee armies advanced to Big and Little Kenesaw in the vicinity of Marietta (Georgia). The Union frontal attacks were repeatedly thrown back with the result that they also had to dig themselves in.

He had, however, to cope with many internal problems.

The Southern states had seceded from the Union in order to maintain their individual rights. A strong central government was nevertheless needed in Richmond for the conduct of the war effort, but the State governors opposed this concept and did their best to sabotage President Davis's measures for centralized administration.

Neither did Davis receive all that much support from his cabinet. Judah Philip Benjamin, one time attorney-general and war minister, and since March 1862, Confederate foreign minister, was one of the key members of the cabinet. Davis relied on him, insofar as his autocratic mood permitted, for the President regarded himself as capable of solving all military and civil problems; he held himself, for example, to be a gifted general. The remainder of the cabinet, however, regarded Benjamin as being too clever by far.

Another capable member was the navy minister

Stephen R. Mallory, who always remained loyal to Davis. He was unable to hinder the blockade with the means at his disposal, but managed to build up a navy from scratch, which in spite of being inferior to the enemy, proved its readiness to fight.

During the existence of the Confederacy there were

Confederate positions at Atlanta.

six war ministers, of whom James A. Seddon managed to last the longest, from November 1862 to February 1865. The others were in office only for short periods as the President tended to see himself in the role of war minister. On the other hand, some of the best men in the South were not represented in the cabinet, especially those who had contributed to the formation of the Confederacy before 1861. Howell Cobb served in the Army as a major-general, and Robert A. Toombs, after a short period as foreign minister, resigned and also served as a general.

Davis wanted a cabinet that would function but not involve itself in politics; he himself would govern and alone!

It was similar in the North, where Lincoln dominated the government, although policy was anchored in the Constitution and his cabinet did contain efficient politicians. Lincoln had still to struggle with individual members, but in contrast to Davis, he understood how to avoid turning rivals into enemies. Several of his colleagues considered themselves as better material for President than Lincoln – who was aware of this – but it did not deter him from using their undoubted talents.

Among these men notably foreign minister William H. Seward and war minister, Edwin M. Stanton (who had replaced Simon Cameron on 15 January 1862) conformed to Lincoln's authority.

But Stanton, who possessed enormous energy, could be very offensive in manner. It was due, however, to his vigour that the Union armies were so well equipped. A man who was very difficult to deal with was Salmon P. Chase, finance minister until July

The Confederate Cabinet. From left to right: Justice Minister Benjamin, the Navy Minister Mallory, the Finance Minister Menninger, Vice-President Stephens, the War Minister Walker, President Davis, the Director-General of the Post Office Reagan and the Minister for Foreign Affairs Toombs.

The Federal cabinet. From left to right: Director-General of the Post Office Blair, the Minister of the Interior Smith, Finance Minister Chase, President Lincoln, the Minister of Foreign Affairs Seward, the War Minister Cameron, the Justice Minister Bates and the Navy Minister Welles.

1864 when Lincoln accepted his resignation. The President was obliged to accept that the latter's disloyalty to him went too far. Comparing the two opposing governments, it may be said that Lincoln received much help from his cabinet in spite of political differences, but Davis received hardly any support at all.

It is a paradox that the Confederate government at first recognizing the rights of the individual states, was to later deny them, especially as far as the Army was concerned. At the beginning of the war, the Confederate soldiers signed on for twelve months service, which meant that the Army would have dis-

solved itself in spring 1862. President Davis immediately introduced a conscription law concerning all males between 18 and 35 years of age (later raised to 45 and finally 50). This measure was bitterly opposed, especially by Georgia, but the law remained in force until the end of the war – although certain exceptions were made which were also subject to vociferous criticism.

On the other hand, the Union did not introduce conscription until 3 March 1863. As we know, the Northern army consisted of regiments that were raised by the individual states, and the volunteers were liable to serve for three years. If new regiments were required as a result of heavy casualties, Washington simply inflicted a recruit quota on each state. If enough volunteers came forward, the extremely unpopular draft laws were not enforced. In order to obtain enough volunteers, sums of money were handed out as bounties – in some cases up to 1,000 dollars. This practice had the great disadvantage that many of those who came forward had not the slightest intention of fighting and often took the first opportunity to desert, in order to volunteer again under a different name. The veterans greatly despised these renegades, who were partly responsible for the fall in morale of the Potomac army in the years 1864–65.

Another recruiting practice that actually invited discontent was the offer of a conscript's freedom from service until the next draft in return for a payment of 300 dollars or the provision of a substitute. These alternatives were particularly hated by the loyal veterans and embittered the poorer classes, who were unable to produce what was for those times, an enormous sum of money.

So as to pacify the recruits of 1861 and 1862, those

On 30 July 1864, a breach was forced in the Confederate lines at Fort Monton by exploding an underground mine. The resulting surprise, however, was not exploited because of the incompetence of the officers concerned.

who signed on for a further three year period were paid a bounty and were permitted to call themselves 'Veteran Volunteers', a title of which they were extremely proud.

Lincoln was a clever politician who was adept at agreeing compromises with those who opposed him. He nevertheless had many difficulties to contend with, especially in 1864 when he was up for re-election. The issue at stake in the election was whether to peacefully conclude the war, or to fight on to the bitter end to preserve the Union. Even a section of his own party, the Republicans, thought that Lincoln was not radical enough, while the Democrats were opposed to the war – they wanted a negotiated peace. Lincoln's chances seemed poor, as the North was suffering the strains of war. Even Grant had been unable to end it, and under his military leadership the casualties mounted in the brutal war of attrition. In Ohio, Illinois and especially New York (13–16 July 1863), civilians rose against the conscription laws, and the Army had to suppress the draft riots with bloodshed; incidents that were remembered with concern when the U.S.

The batteries of Fort Morgan that guarded the entrance to Mobile Bay.

government introduced conscription in the First World War.

The Democrats held their party convention on 29 August in Chicago, and declared that the war had so far failed to unite and strengthen the Union – it would be better to return to the state of affairs that existed before 1861. General McClellan stood as their Presidential candidate, but the Democrats themselves had no real idea how to achieve their aims, as the time for compromise had long since passed.

Lincoln, who was again nominated as candidate on 7 June 1864, was not confident of re-election; he foresaw the complete break-up of the Union.

Apart from the length of hostilities and the high casualties since Grant had assumed the overall command, another reason for strain in the North was the question of the prisoners of war. The inhabitants of the North were greatly occupied by this problem. Prior to 1864 there had been a one for one exchange of prisoners, which was discontinued by Grant when he became Commander-in-Chief. He categorically stopped an exchange on 1 April and again on 18 August 1864. In his view the exchanges only prolonged the war, in that the repatriated prisoners were sorely needed by the South to bolster their forces. The Northern prisoners had perforce to remain in the South, where they died in their thousands in the dreadful conditions in their prison camps. Infamous and feared indeed was the camp at Andersonville in Georgia, where since February 1864, more than 32,000 Union prisoners had been accommodated. But in the North, the Confederate prisoners hardly fared any better, although this was not admitted at the time. On both sides, soldiers who were taken prisoner had to be prepared for the worst, as prisoners' welfare, medical care and hygiene scarcely existed. As a result, 26,436 Southerners and 22,576 Northerners died in captivity. After the war, the commandant of Andersonville, Major Henry Wirtz, was sentenced to death by hanging. This was the only death sentence passed after hostilities had ended, and was the first war crimes trial in history.

Southern agents actively stirred up war-fatigue in the North, and the Confederacy hoped for a rebellion in the Middle-West states. The spokesman there was an obscure secret society known as the Order of American Knights or the Sons of Liberty, who were supporters of the Democratic Party, but whose words were not transformed into deeds. The plans that were hatched were fantastic and completely unrealistic. It was a pure measure of desperation on the part of the Confederacy to get itself involved with such secret societies.

The fall of Atlanta contributed to a raising of morale in the North. Everywhere the Union armies were advancing and the Confederacy was becoming

A Confederate army camp captured by Union troops near Petersburg (24 June 1864).

smaller and smaller. President Davis could no longer hope to avoid a fate that was becoming daily more obvious. The Confederate armies were no longer winning victories that might induce their opponents to sue for peace.

President Lincoln was re-elected on 8 November 1864, receiving 2,213,635 votes, while the Democrats got 1,805,237. Decisive for his victory were the votes of the soldiers, 77·5 per cent. of whom gave him their support.

Total War. General Jubal Early in the Shenandoah Valley still represented a threat to the Union, but nobody had been able to expel him from that important sector.

General Grant accordingly ordered Major-General Philip H. Sheridan – who took command on 7 August 1864 – to defeat Early and to so devastate the Valley that it could no longer be used by the Confederates as a theatre of war. The threat to the communications of the Potomac army had to be ended once and for all, and the Confederates had at

Fort Sunter re-occupied by the Union – the Stars and Stripes were hoisted on 14 April 1865.

all costs to be denied the advantages of fertile agricultural territory.

Sheridan was ordered to so destroy the Valley that even the crows would have nothing to eat. He had 48,000 men at his disposal for the task, including 6,400 cavalry.

Jubal Early had in the meanwhile been reinforced, so that he was able to oppose the Union forces with 25,000 men – which later were reduced to 19,000 men. Sheridan's first task was to reorganize his army and to build up their morale. On 19 September occurred the Battle of Opequonon Creek near Winchester, where the Confederates had to admit defeat with a loss of 4,600 men. Three days later, the Union army was again victorious at Fisher's Hill, and as they set about laying waste to the area, Early withdrew to the south. The destruction was completed by the middle of October, and the Union army took up defensive positions at Cedar Creek – 23 miles south of Winchester.

It was there that Early mounted a surprise attack on 19 October, and succeeded in putting his opponents to flight. Sheridan had just arrived back from a visit to Washington when he encountered the fleeing troops. He was extremely popular with his men, because he always managed to turn up at the right moment. On this occasion he rallied his forces and marched with them back to the front, where a sudden counter-attack totally destroyed the Confederates. The danger had been at last finally eliminated, and all that was left of the enemy were 1,100 men with six guns – who were finally wiped out by Brigadier-General George A. Custer on 2 March 1865.

Following Sherman's occupation of Atlanta, both sides considered their next moves. Sherman ordered the entire civilian population of the town to be evacuated, in order to turn the place into a military

General Sherman and his staff after the capture of Atlanta.

Sherman succeeded in approaching closer and closer to Atlanta by means of continual flanking movements around the Confederate defensive positions. By the middle of July 1864 the town was surrounded and the Battle of Atlanta took place on the 20th of the month. The photograph shows palisades and chevaux desfrises *in the suburbs of the town.*

stronghold – a measure for which he has never been forgiven by the citizens of Georgia.

General Hood thought that by cutting Sherman's communications with Chattanooga, he could force him to retreat or at least to follow him. As a result, there was an engagement at Allatoona to the north of Atlanta on 5 October, but the Confederates failed in their aim and had to retire. Hood then marched to the south to force Sherman to evacuate Atlanta, which the latter had not the slightest intention of doing. Hood's plan was to cross the Tennessee and then advance north – he wanted to regain the State of Tennessee for the Confederacy, in order to be able to advance from Nashville into Kentucky. The operation was daringly conceived, but was born of desperation and a great strategic mistake.

For his part, Sherman believed that there was little point in continuing to occupy Georgia and to lose casualties in defending his lines of communication.

He therefore suggested to Grant the idea of a march to Savannah on the coast, leaving behind everything that was not vitally necessary. The Army would

Demolition of railway lines was one of the main tactics employed by the Union generals during the war.

simply requisition on the way and the countryside would be laid waste – to demonstrate that the Confederacy was no longer able to protect the land and the population, and that in future it depended on the mercy or otherwise of the Union army.

After some initial hesitation, Grant agreed to this controversial plan on 2 November, and Sherman made immediate preparations. The sick and wounded were sent to Chattanooga, as well as all non-effectives. All equipment that could not be carried on the march was abandoned. 68,000 troops were assembled for the march, accompanied by sixty-five guns, 2,500 waggons loaded with ammunition and supplies, and 6000 ambulance carts. In Atlanta itself, everything left was destroyed and the town went up in flames.

The famous march from 'Atlanta to the Sea' began on 15 November 1864.

The Final Events of the War at Sea

The captain had great problems in hiring enough crew members, as by that time few were prepared to risk their lives for the cause of the South.

On the day of her commissioning, the cruiser left Funchal on a course for the Pacific to attempt to destroy the U.S. whaling fleet in the Antarctic. The first ship was taken on 30 October and a further six were sunk in the South Atlantic by the end of the year.

The cruiser arrived then at Melbourne on 25 January, where she remained until 18 February. Waddell had no further success in the South Atlantic as the majority of the whaling fleet had been warned of his presence. The *Shenandoah* managed to destroy four catchers at Lea Harbour on Ascension Island, and the captain found out from captured papers where the others had gone.

Lieutenant Waddell commanded the Confederate auxiliary cruiser Shenandoah *that imposed a series of heavy blows on the American whaling fleet in the Polar Sea, after the war had ended.*

The commerce raider Shenandoah. *After an adventurous voyage along the coast of Siberia, the Captain discovered on 2 August 1865 that the Civil War was already over.*

The end of the war at sea. The final and third most successful Southern commerce raider was the *Shenandoah*, a sailing ship with an auxiliary engine.

The Confederacy bought her from the English in 1864.

She left London on 8 October, supposedly to sail for Bombay, but instead made for Funchal in Madeira, where the steamer *Laurel* was already waiting with the necessary equipment and war stores.

Lieutenant J. I. Waddell commissioned the *Shenandoah* on 19 October. She displaced 1,152 tons, had a speed of nine knots and was armed with four 20-mm. guns, two 32 pdrs. and two 12 pdrs.

Preceding pages. On 5 August 1864 in Mobile Bay, the engagement took place between the Confederate Ironclad Tennessee *and the Union warships commanded by Farragut. The large calibre guns of the monitors damaged the* Tennessee *so severely that she had to lower her flag in surrender.*

The 585-ton Confederate auxiliary cruiser Chickamauga *left port on 28 October 1864, commanded by Lieutenant J. Wilkinson, and took several prizes on the one voyage lasting until 19 November of the same year.*

On 13 April the cruiser set out for the Kuriles (Robert E. Lee had already surrendered at Appomattox Court House on 9 April), and a month later she sailed further north. In the U.S.A. there was great excitement on account of the *Shenandoah* as it was known that she planned to destroy the whaling fleet. On 21 May she was already in the Sea of Okhotsk and six days later encountered the first catcher. She then followed the Siberian coast but had to give up on account of pack ice. On 14 June she left the area and entered the Bering Sea, where, off Cape Nawarin on 14 June, the first catcher was sighted. The hunt began immediately and achieved complete surprise, with the result that Waddell was able to destroy twenty-one ships before 28 June.

This brought the total for the voyage to thirty-three prizes with a value of 1,361,983 dollars.

Waddell again left the area on 5 July and steered for the West Coast of the U.S.A. On 2 August he found out that the Civil War had long been over, a fact that he had already heard from the whalers but had been unwilling to accept. His problem then was to avoid falling into the hands of U.S. warships and being treated as a pirate. Unseen and unhindered, the cruiser managed to reach Liverpool on 6 November, and in spite of protests from Washington, the officers and crew were allowed to go free.

Two further successful auxiliary cruisers were the *Tallahassee* and the *Chickamauga*.

The former, of 500 tons and armed with three guns, operated off the coast of New England in August 1864, captained by John Taylor Wood. Her mission lasted only nineteen days, as the U.S. government was able to hinder her from obtaining more than 100 tons of coal in Canada so that she was forced to return to Wilmington – but not before she had destroyed twenty-three ships.

The *Chickamauga* (685 tons and three guns) set sail on 28 October 1864 commanded by Lieutenant J. Wilkinson, likewise to raid commerce as far afield as the latitude of New York. She only took four prizes but caused great excitement and irritation in U.S. shipping circles.

During the war, the Confederacy fitted out a total of twelve auxiliary cruisers or commerce raiders. In spite of daring voyages and great success, they did not fulfil the expectation that on account of their appearance, the Union would abandon the blockade and go chasing after them. Although the raiders only 135 managed to destroy 5 per cent. of the Northern merchant marine, their activities were significant. As a result of their voyages, nearly half the U.S. ships sailed under other flags and many others did not dare to put to sea. In spite of this, however, the Union trade continued to increase, as neutral flags were still respected.

Blockade runners. Equally surrounded by adventure and romance were the voyages of the blockade runners. It was impossible for the warships of the Union to hermetically seal off the whole of the Confederate coast line. The blockade mainly concentrated on the main Southern harbours – Wilmington (North Carolina), Charleston (South Carolina), Mobile (Alabama), New Orleans and Galveston (Texas) – as only these could be used by deep draught vessels.

After New Orleans was captured, the South had only Wilmington, Charleston and Mobile at their disposal. Wilmington was especially favourably situated and well protected. Forts guarded the entrance at the river mouth which made the maintenance of the

The 900-ton seaworthy Ironclad Stonewall *was built for the Confederacy in France in 1863–4. The warship reached Nassau on 6 May 1865, but had to surrender to the Union in July. The photograph shows her lying in the Potomac.*

blockade more difficult. The most profitable period for the blockade runners was in 1863 and 1864, when enormous benefits were attained, and many English firms participated in the risky enterprises. The main transit stages for goods were Bermuda and Nassau, from where the runners would try to penetrate the watching cordon of warships. Later, special ships were built for the purpose with a low silhouette, high speed and camouflage colours.

If a ship got through, she had to try again on the return run, laden with cotton and tobacco, and a successful trip brought immense profits for the owner. A steamer loaded with, for example, 800 bales of cotton, could earn 420,000 dollars. Even the crews earned ample sums for an adventurous voyage – for instance, the Captain might get 5,000 dollars in gold and the sailors 250 dollars each.

As the main reason for blockade running was the profit motive, the ships brought mostly luxury goods into the South which could be sold with a high margin. The Confederacy thus saw itself forced after 1864, to requisition loading space for military goods.

This step was taken far too late to be able to influence the fate of the South.

During the course of the war, the U.S. Navy created an even finer net in order to trap the runners. They

The wreck of a Confederate blockade runner off Sullivan's Island (South Carolina).

managed to capture or sink 295 steamers, 44 sailing ships and 683 schooners, carrying freight to a total value of 24·5 million dollars. If one adds to this the vessels that were wrecked, the U.S. Navy managed to account for ships to the value of 31·5 million dollars. As the Confederacy had no high seas navy, they were unable to hinder the blockade militarily, but tried to counter it with propaganda about its illegality and lack of success.

The truth, however, was different. The economy of the South suffered greatly and the gold reserves were eaten up by the expensive imports. As a result, only cotton remained as an article for export or barter, and although several million bales were shipped out, this was insufficient to save the economy.

As a further result of the blockade, the prices in the South rocketed. The necessities of daily life either disappeared or could only be obtained at an impossible cost. The troops had enough weapons and ammunition until the end of the war, but lacked more or less everything else. Uniforms and blankets became unobtainable and the grey cloth disappeared almost entirely. The material had to be dyed with peanut colouring, so that in the last years of the conflict, people referred to the 'browns' rather than the 'greys'.

The first modern economic war played its part in reducing the commerce of the South. All efforts to lift the blockade with Ironclads and commerce raiders failed; the South was unable to combat the material superiority of the North.

The capture of Mobile. Mobile lay some thirteen miles from the bay of the same name, the entrance to which was protected by two forts – Morgan and Gaines. The Confederate Admiral Buchanan took command of the defences as the North prepared for its capture. Between the two forts in the 500-yard wide entrance channel he provided underwater obstructions and in addition laid a minefield. The 1,273 ton Ironclad *Tennessee* armed with six guns was transferred to Mobile for use against U.S. warships should they succeed in breaking through past the forts. In addition, the South had a further three wooden gun-boats that had little combat value.

Admiral Farragut commanded the opposing forces, and as in his earlier undertakings, planned to run past the fortifications, this being in his opinion, the best tactics for success.

On 1 August 1864, Brigadier-General R. S. Granger arrived with 2,400 soldiers to attack Fort Gaines.

Admiral Farragut had eighteen warships available, four of which were monitors – his flagship was the famous *Hartford*.

At 05.30 hours on 5 August, the ships formed into two columns and approached the entrance. An hour later the monitors opened the bombardment, to be followed by the other vessels. At this point the *Tennessee*, accompanied by the three gun-boats, steered for the wooden Union vessels. The monitors

The surrender of the Tennessee *on 5 August 1864.*

The famous 2,900-ton U.S. cruiser Hartford *took part in the capture of New Orleans in April 1862 where she was the flagship of Farragut. During the Vicksburg campaign under General Grant she anchored off the fortress, and gained further fame in the engagement in Mobile Bay on 5 August 1864.*

immediately altered course, whereby the *Tecumseh* hit a mine and sank. In the engagement with the Ironclad, several of the Union ships were slightly damaged, but she could not prevent the breakthrough – the mines had not fulfilled their purpose.

The *Tennessee* reappeared at 08.45 hours, and the monitors took up the challenge that was to prove one of the hardest engagements of the Civil War.

The cruisers rammed the Ironclad several times without effect, but the 11-in. and 15-in. guns of the monitors damaged her so severely that she was forced to capitulate.

The warships then continued with their bombardment of the forts, which hoisted white flags on 21 August. This meant that Mobile was isolated and could no longer be used by blockade runners, although the town itself was not occupied by Union troops until 21 March 1865.

Scorched Earth

Sherman's march to the Sea. The Confederacy had no significant forces with which to oppose Sherman's march. His army advanced across country in an arc some 67 miles wide, and it seemed more like a country rampage to the soldiers. Anything that could be of any use to the South was destroyed – bridges, railway equipment, factories, barns, farms etc. As the army was living off the land, detachments were sent out each morning to requisition food supplies, and the troops lived to excess as more was procured than was really needed. The situation was exploited by marauders, not only from the Union, but from the Confederate side as well.

These underworld elements plundered, stole and robbed whenever they had a chance, and although Sherman could well have put a stop to their activities, he refrained as they were fulfilling his purpose of laying Georgia waste.

The Confederacy was powerless, although General Hood tried to halt the march by raiding into Tennessee. By that stage of the war, however, the Union enjoyed such a superiority that they could have dispensed with Sherman's force.

General Hood's army destroyed. The Confederate army started off for the north in the direction of Nashville on 19 November 1864. General John M. Schofield was forced to retire slowly from South Tennessee in the face of the 54,000 advancing Southerners. At Spring Hill, Hood and his cavalry almost succeeded in cutting off the retreat of Schofield's army, but the Confederates under Forrest were forced back and their opponents escaped from the trap. Hood had lost a unique chance to defeat the Union force.

On 30 November, Schofield prepared to defend himself at Franklin. The same afternoon, still angry about his lack of success, Hood attacked the well prepared enemy positions frontally with 38,000 men.

At a cost of 6,300 men – including five generals, the useless assault had to be abandoned, while their opponents suffered only 2,300 casualties. During the night, Schofield withdrew in the direction of

Major-General John McAllister Schofield, the commander of the Ohio army, played a decisive role in the success of the Union in Georgia.

Nashville before the numerically superior enemy, while Hood followed hard on his heels.

Nashville was one of the largest Union fortresses, and to assault it would have been a waste of time. Hood camped to the south of the town and waited.

Just what he intended to do, he did not know himself; then his situation became hopeless. He could not storm the defences, he could not advance any further and he could hardly retire south again. There was no way out of his position and he was doomed to failure. The advance had been a big mistake on the part of the Confederacy, as a retreat was bound to collapse into a catastrophe, especially as the troops no longer had any confidence in their general.

In Washington in the meanwhile, there was worry over the fact that an enemy army was operating so far into Union territory and that General Thomas hesitated to attack it. Grant wanted to sack Thomas and concern himself with the seemingly critical situation at Nashville. Snowstorms, however, made a Union attack impossible for a while, but on 15 December, Thomas assaulted and threw the enemy back. The following day he continued the offensive, and for the first time in the whole Civil War, the Union managed to totally destroy a Confederate army.

Sherman in Savannah. In the meanwhile, Sherman had continued undisturbed his march to the coast.

Washington was anxious, as nobody had any idea where his army was or if it had been successful, but Grant managed again and again to calm the President's fears. On 9 December, Sherman was near Savannah, and four days later, Fort McAllister at the mouth of the Ogeechee River was stormed in order to provide a base on the Atlantic coast and to establish communication with the Navy. Savannah was defended by some 15,000 men under Lieutenant-General Hardee, who withdrew, however, to avoid being cut off from his lines of communication. Sherman failed to take the opportunity of attacking Hardee and his small army, and let him get away.

The Union troops marched into the town on 21 December, and General Sherman presented it to Lincoln as a Christmas present.

The capture of Fort Fisher. The capture of Fort Fisher is reckoned to be one of the greatest amphib-

A fallen Confederate soldier in the vicinity of Spotsylvania Court House.

ious operations carried out by the U.S. Navy during the Civil War. Right to the end of the war, Wilmington remained the most important harbour for the Southern blockade runners, and could not be eliminated without occupying Cape Fear. Ever since 1862, the Confederacy had been building Fort Fisher on the north-east point of the entrance, and it was one of the most powerful of their forts. On account of its extent and lay-out, it was regarded as being almost impregnable, and due to navigational problems, it could not simply be bombarded by warships. The only chance to deal with the fort was by a combined land and sea attack.

It was not until the end of 1864 that the North began to seriously consider such an operation, especially as General Lee would be cut off from all further supplies once Wilmington fell.

Admiral David D. Porter took command of the Atlantic Blockading Squadron on 12 October 1864, and immediately began to assemble the necessary ships for the bombardment and landing. Navy Minister Welles did everything to ensure that the operation would be a success.

In command of the landing force was Major-General Benjamin F. (Ben) Butler, who delayed the operation, however. He believed that he could eliminate the fort by means of a ship loaded with explosive. During the night of 23–24 December, the *Louisiana* crammed with 253 tons of gunpowder, blew up, but failed to take the fort with her – the garrison did not even notice the explosion.

On 24 December, the monitors and the other warships – it was the largest assembly of vessels during the Civil War – commenced the bombardment. The following day the troops landed near Fort Fisher but were unable to advance through the Confederate fire. In spite of the massive cannonade, the fortifications were still intact, and General Butler re-embarked his troops and returned to Hampton Roads. In his view the fort could only be captured after a lengthy siege, but all he got for his pains was to be immediately relieved of his command.

During the two day bombardment, the ships commanded by Admiral Porter had fired more than 20,000 shells (*circa* 600 tons), but the fort itself had been hardly damaged – only three guns were dismounted.

143

The casemates of Fort Fisher, the objective of a large landing operation carried out by the Union army at the end of 1864.

Major-General A. J. Terry assumed command of the landing force, and on 12 January, forty-four ships, among which were the heavily armed monitors, took on their assigned targets. The bombardment continued through the night into the following day, and on 15 January, 2,000 sailors and marines went ashore to try to take the fort from the sea side. The first storm was beaten back with heavy casualties, but Colonel William Lamb, the garrison commander assumed that this was the prelude to the main attack from the same direction. He moved reinforcements to the sea side, with the result that General Terry was able to enter the fort from the land side and take possession of part of the impregnable fortress. The following day the Confederates blew up the remaining fortifications and evacuated the whole complex.

Union gun-boats immediately entered the Wilmington channel where they found and captured several blockade runners, although the town was not occupied until 22 February 1865.

Fighting on the James River. At the beginning of 1865 there was further fighting with Confederate Ironclads. The *Virginia*, *Richmond* and *Fredericksburg* accompanied by six gun-boats and two torpedo boats (Davids), attacked the large supply depot of the Potomac army at City Point on 23

Fort Fisher, which guarded the blockade runner harbour of Wilmington (North Carolina), was regarded as being impregnable, but it fell on 15 January 1865.

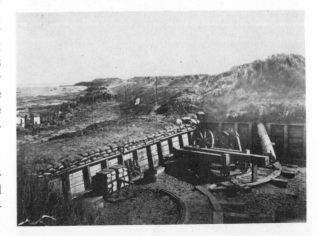

January. The plan was to afford the hard-pushed army at Petersburg a brief respite, but with the exception of the *Fredericksburg*, none of the vessels were able to break through the Union barrier. The Confederate flotilla was fired upon by artillery, which was aided the following day by the guns of a monitor. In spite of suffering heavy damage, the Confederate units were able to make their escape, and after the fall of Richmond, the flotilla on the James, commanded by Rear-Admiral Raphael Semmes, was blown up and scuttled.

The final engagements in 1864. As the year 1864 approached its end, it was clear to all concerned that the struggle could not last for much longer. The Confederacy no longer had an intact army with which to oppose her victorious opponents. The Rebs were unable to halt Sherman's march to the sea and Lee was pinned down by Grant in Petersburg.

In Tennessee, 12,000 Union cavalry were preparing to advance into Alabama. They were armed with the latest repeater rifles, the rate of fire of which exceeded anything that had thus far been used during the war.

All that the Confederacy consisted of territorially at that time was Carolina and the south of Virginia.

A locomotive belonging to the U.S. Military Railroad at City Point. A special track was laid to the trenches at Petersburg to transport food, munitions etc.

Unconditional Surrender

Preceding pages. On 2 April 1865, the Confederates had to evacuate their capital. The following day it was occupied by U.S. cavalry, but during the evacuation it was partly destroyed by fire.

The end of the war. On 11 February 1865, General Sherman with 60,000 battle-tested veterans set off to march north, with the intention of joining up with General Schofield and a further 23,000 troops in North Carolina. The Confederacy recalled Johnston, who, with 40,000 men was to try to halt Sherman, but his force no longer possessed the necessary fighting spirit and reserves.

The danger was recognized in Richmond, and on 3 February, Lee was appointed Commander-in-Chief of all forces, but even he could no longer save the situation.

The Southern strategists hoped that Sherman in South Carolina would be hindered by the many small streams that were flooded in winter, as well as the marshy ground and the bad roads. Many of his soldiers, however, were frontiersmen who were used to such conditions, and the march continued undisturbed.

South Carolina suffered terribly from the plundering and burnings carried out by the invading troops, who felt that as this state had started the war it should be made to feel their special sense of revenge.

In March 1865, it was decided in Richmond to arm the Negroes – a step that was taken far too late. The government also tried to gain recognition in London and Paris by announcing the abolition of

On 28 March 1864, President Lincoln conferred with the Generals Grant and Sherman on board the River Queen *at City Point. On the right is Rear-Admiral Porter. At this famous conference, Lincoln stated his policy of ending the war with as little bloodshed as possible, and after it was over, of following a liberal policy towards the conquered Southern States.*

slavery. At that time, however, neither England nor France had the slightest intention of recognizing the Confederacy that was approaching total collapse.

President Davis put out peace feelings to Washington. On 3 February on a Union steamer in Hampton Roads, the Confederate Vice-President Alexander Stephens, R. M. T. Hunter, who was at that time President of the Senate and Judge John A. Campbell, met President Lincoln and Foreign Minister Seward. Lincoln was not prepared to make any concessions. First, the Confederate army had to be dissolved and the autonomy of the Union restored in the South, before peace could be further discussed. This meant unconditional surrender. Lincoln had liberal views and had no intention of insisting on punishment or other repressive measures. There were, however, plenty of hotheads in Congress in Washington who dreamed only of revenge and repression.

Sherman's troops occupied Columbia, the capital of South Carolina, on 17 February 1865. The following night the town went up in flames, although who was responsible has never been satisfactorily established.

The meeting broke up without result. The Confederacy had to be outfought to the bitter end by military means.

Sherman continued his march, and occupied Columbia, the capital of South Carolina on 17 February. The same day, the Southerners evacuated Charleston, that had thus far remained inviolable from the sea side. Since 14 April, the Stars and Stripes had flown once more over Fort Sumter, having been hoisted in the presence of Major-General Robert Anderson.

From Columbia, Sherman moved into North Carolina, where little damage was done.

From Petersburg to Appomattox Court House. The Union positions around Petersburg stretched in a 43-mile long semi-circle, the northern end of which was near Richmond and the other to the southwest of Petersburg where it cut the railway line. General Lee believed that he still had a chance to defeat the Union army. His plan was to try to disengage from Grant without being noticed, then to join up with Johnston's force in North Carolina to attack Sherman, before returning to deal with Grant.

Bomb-proof dugout behind the front lines at Petersburg.

Specially picked troops would attack the Union centre, so that Grant would be forced to weaken his left wing to protect the railway, and thus avoid being cut off. The Confederates hoped to break through the centre and then march off to the south. The reason that the plan failed to work was that the 60,000 Southerners were opposed by 105,000 Union troops around Richmond and Petersburg.

At dawn on 25 March, the Confederates commanded by General John B. Gordon stormed forward for the last time. They captured Fort Stedman and managed to get through to the railway line, but the offensive was broken. The Union defensive positions were too strong, and towards mid-day the attackers were back in their own trenches.

In the meanwhile, Grant had realized that it would be impossible to mount a frontal attack against the equally well constructed enemy positions, even taking into account his numerical superiority. Instead,

he lengthened his lines further to the west, so that less Confederate soldiers would be available for each yard of trench. Lee was thus forced either to abandon the Petersburg position or to offer battle, which he could not win on account of the disparity in numbers.

The Union army attacked the Confederate right wing on 31 March, but as was to be expected, were thrown back with heavy casualties. Since 26 March, Sheridan had joined the Potomac army with 12,000 cavalry from the Shenandoah Valley, and he moved to Dinwiddie Court House where a hefty engagement broke out between the two sides. From there he rode to Five Forks to occupy the railway line leading to the south. If he could hold Five Forks, then the Union army had interspersed itself between Lee and Johnston, and Petersburg and Richmond would have to be evacuated. On 1 April, Sheridan attacked the Confederates there who were commanded by General George Pickett, and totally defeated them, taking 3,200 prisoners.

Then Grant took the initiative. On 2 April he broke through the Confederate centre at Petersburg,

The ruins of Richmond. The fall of the Confederate capital brought the end of the war in sight.

whereby the Southern General A. P. Hill was killed. The same evening, Richmond and Petersburg were evacuated and the government fled, while Lee marched west with 40,000 men to try to join up with Johnston. He could, however, no longer turn south, as Sheridan blocked his way and forced him further west. The Confederate army only managed to march on account of their unshakable confidence in Lee – ration issues had become scarce. On 6 April, the Union attacked the Confederate rearguard at Sayler's Creek, and managed to destroy their ration and ammunition carts. Ewell surrendered with 4,000 men, and Anderson with a further 2,000. The Southern army had more or less ceased to exist, and

Major-General Richard S. Ewell who was regarded as one of the most capable of Lee's generals. Although wounded, he fought on resolutely, but had to surrender on 6 April 1865.

151

A Union pontoon bridge over the Appomattox at Petersburg in May 1865.

realized the awful consequences of irregular warfare, and Grant believed that with the end of hostilities, the Southerners would find recognition once again as loyal U.S. citizens. His conditions therefore were simple – the soldiers should surrender their arms and give their word not to fight any longer. In that case, they would be allowed to go home, and to participate in the rebuilding of the nation. If they were prepared to do this, they would not be prosecuted by the Federal authorities. After a final parade, a total of 28,356 officers and men laid down their weapons.

In North Carolina, there had been an engagement between Johnston and Sherman at Bentonville from 19–21 March, but the Confederates were unable to turn the situation to their favour. When Johnston heard of Lee's surrender, he realized that he had no other alternative, and he capitulated with 37,047 men on 18 April.

In the areas remaining to the Confederacy there was no longer any question of carrying on the struggle.

In Alabama, the U.S. cavalry occupied one town after another. Mobile fell, and Confederate forces fought on only to the west of the Mississippi.

The building in Appomattox Court House where Grant and Lee met on 9 and 10 April 1865.

in those last days Lee had less than 30,000 men to lead. On 9 April, the Union had overtaken and surrounded the Confederate troops at the small settlement of Appomattox Court House. Lee's further advance was blocked, and a junction with Johnston could no longer be contemplated under the circumstances. There was no longer even a chance for the Southerners to achieve even a partial success, as they had reached the end of their endurance – less than half of them had weapons and ammunition.

On the morning of 9 April, the Confederates attacked for the last time before the main enemy army had arrived, but when it put in an appearance, the assault was stopped and Lee was informed of the situation. As the Union army was about to advance, a Confederate representative marched forward with a white flag. A deathly hush settled over the battlefield but the soldiers just could not believe that the war was over.

General U. S. Grant and General Robert E. Lee met as a result in the living room of a house belonging to Mr Wilmer McLean in Appomattox Court House. Lee had to decide whether to dissolve the Army and fight a guerrilla war, or to surrender. Lee, however,

152

General Robert E. Lee at the front door of his house in Richmond. The photograph was taken by the well known war photographer Mathew Brady, a few days after Lee had surrendered.

On 4 May, General Richard Taylor surrendered Alabama and Mississippi, and Kirby Smith's army to the west of the river laid down its arms on 26 May.

President Davis and his cabinet wanted to escape to the western territories and there continue the war, but this was pointless, and in view of the general situation, the cabinet dissolved itself. Davis was taken prisoner on 10 May at Irwinsville in Georgia, and was brought to Fort Monroe.

The end, and a new beginning. The actual hostilities were over, but President Lincoln was confronted with the problem of how the peace was to become a reality. He was convinced that both sides were responsible for the start of the conflict, and thus for its cost. Thus he reasoned that both sides must share the victory, that must be so concluded that both North and South would feel that they had gained something from it. Such a peace did not envisage any sort of punishment of the Southerners, which Lincoln had always refused to consider, but there would be no restoration of institutions such as slavery already abolished by the war.

Lincoln hoped that the Confederate armies would simply dissolve of their own accord and that the soldiers would go home. As soon as possible, civilian government would be installed in the secessionist states, although it would be difficult to readmit them to the Union and to restore civil and political rights.

A great measure of political understanding and feeling was needed to solve such difficult problems, and Lincoln had no intention of relinquishing his right to deal with them.

The murder of Lincoln, however, put an end to these extremely liberal proposals. The actor Wilkes Booth shot him in his box at Ford's Theatre in Washington on 14 April, and the following day he died from his wounds.

Following the death of Lincoln, the radical Republicans came to power, who wanted just the opposite of what he had planned. The new President, Andrew Johnson, was surrounded by men who thought only in terms of punishment and revenge. Because of this, the rumour was spread about in the North that Lincoln had been murdered by agents of Jefferson Davis – which was absolute nonsense, especially as the Southern position could only become worse as a result of his death. War Minister Stanton was one of those who became adept at exploiting the suspicious mood created by the cowardly assassination, and so manipulating public opinion that for the next few years North and South regarded each other with bitterness and hatred. The period of reconstruction began, characterized by many injustices and without providing a lasting solution to the Negro problem – the latter was simply pushed to one side and ignored.

The results of the war. The losses in the war were terribly high, although exact statistics are not available, as the Confederacy failed to produce any reliable figures.

67,058 Union soldiers fell in battle, while the Confederate figures vary between 80,000 and 90,000. 43,021 Northern soldiers died of their wounds, and a shocking number died of sickness – 224,586 men, while the Confederates lost some 160–180,000 from the same cause.

There was no question of medical treatment as we 153

This photograph, taken in April 1865 at Petersburg, gives a good impression of the wretched condition of the Southern States at the end of the Civil War.

understand it. The doctors did their best, but even that was not enough, and only a few of them understood why wounds became infected or the reasons why illnesses developed. As a result, treatment was primitive, and if a wound was bandaged, it should suppurate according to the doctors of the time. Sterilization was unknown and the surgical instruments were simply washed in water.

It is hardly to be wondered at that sanitary conditions in the army camps were indescribable, and thousands of soldiers from both sides were affected by typhus, malaria, pneumonia, dysentery etc. Water was considered drinkable just so long as it did not smell rotten. Nurses did not exist during the early war years as it was not considered fitting for men to be cared for by women.

Slavery had been abolished and the Negroes were free to make decisions, but in practice they simply obeyed new masters. Their situation hardly improved, so that they remained poor and nobody bothered about training them to earn a living.

The cost of the conflict was higher for the Americans than was incurred in the First World War. Union loans and taxes came to not less than three thousand million dollars, while the Confederacy had borrowed two thousand million. The economic basis of the South had been almost totally destroyed, and the final losses for both sides came to some twenty thousand million dollars. The burden of the Civil War had to be carried right on into the twentieth century.

The reconstruction of the South (1865–77) and the readmission of the Southern states into the Union created bad blood, as the radical Republicans thought only in terms of punishing the rebels. It took until 1870 for the last Secession state to be readmitted, and in the meanwhile the South was embittered by the setting up of five military districts.

The Generals ran their governments and issued their orders at bayonet point.

In addition, the white population of the South was forced to accept not only the 14th Amendment to the Constitution, whereby the Negroes would enjoy the same civil rights, but also the 15th Amendment that gave them the right to vote. As the majority of the Negroes were illiterate, the situation was exploited by the so-called 'carpet-baggers' who with the help of Coloured votes tried to set up new governments in the South. These administrations, in which black illiterates served, were more or less incompetent and corrupt. They wasted money, most of which flowed into their own pockets and raised taxes in order to ruin the whites. The South, as a result, became poorer than it had been as an immediate consequence of the war.

The white population finally resisted this regime by

force (Ku Klux Klan) and by intimidation. The old political machinery of the Democratic Party at last reawakened and captured power in the Southern states by peaceful means.

In 1877, the last Federal troops were recalled from Louisiana, Florida and South Carolina. One of the results of Northern rule over the South was the creation of race hatred. The solution to this problem has still not been found in the U.S.A.

The damage inflicted by the U.S. monitors on Charleston is a symbol of the dislocation and total defeat of the South.

Bibliography

General works

Alan Baker, The Civil War in America (London 1961)

Pierre Belperron, La guerre de sécession 1861–1865 (Paris 1973)

Henri Bernard, La guerre de sécession des Etats-Unis 1861–1865 (Brussels 1973)

Mark M. Boatner, The Civil War Dictionary (New York 1959)

Bruce Catton, The Centennial History of the Civil War, 3 vols (Garden City, N.Y. 1961–1965)

Bruce Catton, This Hallowed Ground (Garden City, N.Y. 1956)

Bruce Catton, The Penguin Book of the American Civil War (London 1967)

Robert Cruden, The War that never ended (Englewood Cliffs, N. J. 1973)

Ernest Dupuy and Trevor N. Dupuy, The Compact History of the Civil War (New York 1960)

Robert H. Jones, Disrupted Years: the Civil War and Reconstruction Years (New York 1973)

E. B. Long, The Civil War Day by Day: an Almanac 1861–1865 (Garden City, N. Y. 1971)

Ralph Newman and E. B. Long, The Civil War Digest (New York 1960)

Roy F. Nichols, The States of Power, 1845–1877 (New York 1961)

Peter J. Parish, The American Civil War (London 1975)

James G. Randall and David Donald, The Civil War and Reconstruction (Boston 1969)

James A. Rawley, Turning Points of the Civil War (Lincoln, Neb. 1965)

Emory M. Thomas, The American War and Peace 1860–1877 (Englewood Cliffs, N. J. 1973)

The Civil War in pictures

John C. Blay, The Civil War, a pictorial Profile (New York 1958)

Lamont Buchanan, A pictorial History of the Confederacy (New York 1951)

Bruce Catton, American Heritage picture History of the Civil War (New York 1960)

David Donald (ed), Divided we fought: a pictorial History of the War 1861–1865 (New York 1952)

Alexander Gardner, Photographic Sketch Book of the Civil War (New York 1959)

James D. Horan, Mathew Brady: Historian with a Camera (New York 1955)

Renée Lemaître, La guerre de sécession en photos (Brussels 1975)

Hirst D. Milholen and J. Johnson, Best Photos of the Civil War (New York 1961)

Fletcher Pratt, Civil War in Pictures (Garden City, N. Y. 1957)

Bell I. Wiley and Hirst D. Milholen, They who fought here (New York 1959)

The causes of the Civil War

Avery O. Craven, The Coming of the Civil War (New York 1957)

Jean Heffer, Les origines de la guerre de sécession (Paris 1971)

Edwin C. Rozwenc (ed), The Causes of the American Civil War (Boston 1972)

Kenneth M. Stamp (ed), The Causes of the Civil War (Englewood Cliffs, N. J. 1974)

Hans L. Trefousse (ed), The Causes of the Civil War (New York 1971)

Politics and diplomacy

Lynn M. Case and Warren F. Spencer, The United States and France: Civil War Diplomacy (Philadelphia 1970)

E. Merton Coulter, The Confederate States of America 1861–1865 (Baton Rouge, La. 1950)

Glyndon G. van Deusden, William Henry Seward (New York 1967)

Don E. Fehrenbacher (ed), The leadership of Abraham Lincoln (New York 1970)

Norman A. Graebner, The enduring Lincoln (Urbana, Ill. 1959)

Reinhard H. Luthin, The real Abraham Lincoln (Englewood Cliffs, N. J. 1960)

Allan Nevins, The Statesmanship of the Civil War (New York 1953)

Frank L. Owsley, King Cotton Diplomacy: Foreign Relations of the Confederate States of America (Chicago 1959)

Rembert W. Patrick, Jefferson Davis and his Cabinet (Baton Rouge, La. 1944)

James G. Randall and Richard N. Current, Lincoln the President, 4 vols (New York 1944–55)

James A. Rawley (ed), Lincoln and Civil War Politics (New York 1969)

J. W. Schulte Nordholt, Abraham Lincoln (Arnhem 1959)

Hudson Strode, Jefferson Davis, 3 vols (New York 1955–1964)

F. E. Vandiver, Their tattered Flags (New York 1970)

The Civil War generals

Ned Bradford, Battles and Leaders of the Civil War (New York 1956)

Bruce Catton, Grant moves South (Boston 1960)

Bruce Catton, Grant takes Command (Boston 1969)

Freeman Cleaves, Meade of Gettysburg (Norman, Okla. 1960)

J. F. C. Fuller, Grant and Lee: a Study in Personality and Generalship (London 1933)

Warren W. Hassler, George B. McClellan: the Man who saved the Union (Baton Rouge, La. 1957)

Richard Harwell, R. E. Lee (New York 1961)

Basil H. Liddell Hart, Sherman: Soldier, Realist, American (New York 1929)

F. A. Lord, Lincoln's Railroad Man: Herman Haupt (Rutherford, N. J. 1969)

James L. McDonough, Schofield: Union General in the Civil War and Reconstruction (Tallahassee, Fla. 1972)

Frank E. Vandiver, Mighty Stonewall (New York 1957)

Ezra J. Warner, Generals in blue: Lives of the Union Commanders (Baton Rouge, La. 1964)

Ezra J. Warner, Generals in gray: Lives of the Confederate Commanders (Baton Rouge, La. 1959)

T. Harry Williams, Lincoln and his Generals (New York 1952)

T. Harry Williams, P. G. T. Beauregard: Napoleon in gray (Baton Rouge, La. 1955)

The war at sea

Bern Anderson, By Sea and by River: The Naval History of the Civil War (New York 1962)

Robert Carse, Blockade: The Civil War at Sea (New York 1958)

Hamilton Cochran, Blockade Runners of the Confederacy (Indianapolis 1958)

Frank R. Donavan, Ironclads of the Civil War (New York 1964)

Virgil C. Jones, The Civil War at Sea, 3 vols. (New York 1960–62)

Charles L. Lewis, David Glasgow Farragut, 2 vols. (Annapolis, Md 1941–43)

Clarence E. Macartney, Mr. Lincoln's Admirals (New York 1956)

James M. Merrill, The Rebel Shore: the Story of Union Sea Power in the Civil War (Boston 1957)

John D. Milligan, Gunboats down the Mississippi (Annapolis, Md 1965)

R. S. West, Mr. Lincoln's Navy (New York 1957)

Social and economic aspects

Robert C. Black, The Railroads of the Confederacy (Chapel Hill, N. C. 1952)

Alfred H. Bill, The beleaguered City: Richmond 1861–1865 (New York 1946)

Clement Eaton, The Waning of the old South Civilization (Athens, Ga. 1968)

Emerson David Fite, Social and Industrial Condition in the North during the Civil War (New York 1950)

John H. Franklin, The Emancipation Declaration (New York 1963)

Bray Hammond, Sovereignty and an empty Purse: Banks and Politics in the Civil War (Princeton 1970)

Benjamin Quarles, Lincoln and the Negro (New York 1962)

Benjamin Quarles, The Negro in the Civil War (Boston 1953)

Charles W. Ramsdell, Behind the Lines in the Southern Confederacy (Baton Rouge, La. 1944)

George W. Smith and Charles Judah (ed), Life in the North during the Civil War: a Source History (Albuquerque 1966)

Thomas Weber, The Northern Railroads in the Civil War 1861–1865 (New York 1952)

Richard C. Todd, Confederate Finance (Athens, Ga. 1954)

Bell I. Whiley, The Plain People of the Confederacy (Baton Rouge, La. 1943)

Defeat and victory

Bruce Catton, A Stillness at Appomattox (Garden City, N. Y. 1953)

Henry S. Commager (ed), The Defeat of the Confederacy (Princeton 1964)

Avery O. Craven, Reconstruction: the Ending of the Civil War (New York 1969)

David Donald (ed), Why the North won the Civil War (Baton Rouge, La. 1960)

Martin E. Mantell, Johnson, Grant and the Politics of Reconstruction (New York 1973)

Kenneth M. Stamp, The Era of Reconstruction 1865–1877 (New York 1965)

Richard Taylor, Destruction and Reconstruction (New York 1955)

Charles H. Wesley, The Collapse of the Confederacy (Washington 1922)

Bell I. Wiley, The Road to Appomattox (Memphis 1956)

Illustration Sources

PE

OHIO

ILLINOIS

• Indianapolis

• Pittsb

• Harp

• Cincinatti

INDIANA

Rich Mountain

• Westport

• Boonville

• St. Louis

Missouri

Harrisonburg

• Louisville

WEST
VIRGINIA

Ohio

MISSOURI

KENTUCKY

• Perryville

Lynchbu

Bowling Green

Cumberland

• Mill Springs

VIRGINIA

• Wilson's Creek

Island 10

• Paducah

• Franklin

• Knoxville

Greensb

Fort Donelson

• Pea Ridge

Fort Pillow

• Nashville

Fort
Henry

NORTH CAROLINA

• Prairie Grove

Fort Randolph

• Murfreesboro

Grand Junction

TENNESSEE

• Chattanooga

ARKANSAS

• Memphis

• Shiloh

1865

• Chickamauga

• Corinth

Tennessee

• Helena

• Iuka

• Resaca

• Columbia

1862·3

Mississippi

• Tupelo

• Marietta

SOUTH
CAROL

• Atlanta

• Columbus

• Augusta

MISSISSIPPI

ALABAMA

Savannah

• Milledgeville

• Charlesto

1864

TEXAS

• Selma

• Macon

LOUISIANA

• Vicksburg

• Jackson

• Meridian

Po

• Savannah

Fort F

• Champion's Hill

Fort McAllister

• Alexandria

• Montgomery

GEORGIA

• Baton Rouge

• Mobile

Alabama

• Pensacola

• Fernandi

1862·3

• Jacksonville

• Olustee

• Galveston

New Orleans

• St. Au

Fort St. Philip

Fort Jackson

FLORIDA

WEST GULF SQUADRON

EAST GULF SQUADRON